Daily Lenten Meditations

Prayerful reflections from John Paul II

EDITED BY FR. MAX POLAK

LITURGY
TRAINING
PUBLICATIONS

Dedicatory:

Ad maiorem gloriam Redemptoris hominis et Matris eius
Hobart, October 28, 2003-10-29

Editor's note

The season of Lent is a time when many Catholics and other Christians are drawn to deeper reflection and special acts of prayer and worship. For Catholics, it may mean, among other things, attending the Eucharistic Sacrifice more frequently, even every day. Whether or not this is their choice, the present volume is designed to meet a need often felt by them and by Christians of all traditions for stimulating spiritual reading.

Excerpts taken from the homilies, addresses and official letters of Pope John Paul II's long and generous evangelising activity have been put together to form a kind of spiritual pilgrimage over the course of Lent. The texts have been chosen to help readers, day by day, consider, examine themselves or pray over a theme that is relevant to Lent's call to faith and conversion.

The path followed has as its guideposts the Church's selection of readings for the Masses of Lent, especially the Gospel of the day. A theme coming out of the readings is announced. The readings are then listed together with their headings. There follows a highlighted phrase, generally from the Gospel, that in nearly all cases will be found commented on or incorporated somewhere in the Pope's reflection. This method is intended to be particularly helpful to Catholic readers who wish to remain in tune with the Lenten liturgy. Other Christians, however, should find that this format allows for ample meditation on the Scriptures. Since the Biblical texts are not actually reproduced, some may wish to keep a Bible or missal close at hand.

Fr. Max Polak

Published in The USA and Canada by **Liturgy Training Publications,**
Archdiocese of Chicago, 1800 North Hermitage Avenue, Chicago, Illinois, 60622-1101. **USA ISBN 1-56854-530-4**

First Published in England by **Gracewing,**
2 Southern Ave, Leominster, Herefordshire, HR6 0QF. **UK ISBN 0-85244-278-5**

Published in Australia and New Zealand by **Little Hills Press Pty. Ltd.,**
Unit 3, 18 Bearing Road, Seven Hills, NSW 2147, www.littlehills.com.
AUS ISBN 1-86315-219-9

Contents

Ash Wednesday

The heart of Lent

Readings of the day
Joel 2:12-18 *Let your hearts be broken, not your garments torn.*
2 Corinthians 5:20-6:2 *Be reconciled to God, now is the acceptable time.*
Matthew 6:1-6. 16-18 *Your Father, who sees all that is done in secret will reward you.*

Psalm 50 "Create in me a clean heart, O God, and put a new and right spirit within me" (Ps 51 [50]:10).

In a certain sense, these words of the responsorial psalm contain the very heart of Lent and, at the same time, express its essential program. The words are taken from the Miserere, the psalm in which the sinner opens his heart to God, confesses his guilt and implores forgiveness for his sins: "Wash me thoroughly from my iniquity, and cleanse me from my sin! For I know my transgressions and my sin is ever before me. Against you, against you only, have I sinned and done that which is evil in your sight… Cast me not away from your presence and take not your Holy Spirit from me" (Ps 51, 2-4; 11).

This psalm is an unusually effective liturgical commentary on the Rite of Ashes. Ashes are a sign of man's transience and subjection to death. In this season, when we are preparing to relive liturgically the mystery of the Redeemer's death on the cross, we must more deeply feel and experience our own mortality. We are mortal beings, yet our death does not mean destruction and annihilation. In it, God has inscribed the profound hope of the new creation. Thus the sinner who celebrates Ash Wednesday can and must cry: "Create in me a clean heart, O God, and put a new and right spirit within me" (ibid., 12). *Ash Wednesday*

Homily, February 12, 1997.

With this in mind we begin our Lenten journey, taking up the spirit of the great Jubilee that marked an extraordinary time of repentance and reconciliation for the entire Church. It was a year of intense spiritual fervour in which God's mercy was poured abundantly on the world… The journey to which Lent invites us takes place above all in prayer: Christian communities must become authentic "schools of prayer" in these weeks. Another important objective is helping the faithful to approach the sacrament of Reconciliation, so that everyone may "rediscover Christ as *mysterium pietatis,* the one in whom God shows us his compassionate heart and reconciles us fully with himself" (*Novo millennio ineunte,* n.37). Moreover, the experience of God's mercy cannot fail to inspire the commitment to charity, spurring the Christian community to "stake everything on charity" (cf. *Novo millennio ineunte,* IV). In the school of Christ, the community better understands the demanding preferential option for the poor, which is a "testimony to God's love, to his providence and mercy" (ibid.).

"Be reconciled to God!" (2 Cor 5:20) …These words insistently echo in our spirit. Today – the liturgy tells us – is the "acceptable time" for our reconciliation with God. With this in mind, we will receive ashes and take the first steps of our Lenten journey. Let us generously continue on this road, keeping our eyes firmly set on Christ crucified. For the Cross is humanity's salvation: only by starting from the Cross is it possible to build a future of hope and peace for everyone. *Ash Wednesday Homily, February 28, 2001*

Thursday after Ash Wednesday

The way of conversion

Readings of the day
Deuteronomy 30:15-20 *I set before you life or death, blessing or curse.*
Psalm 1 *Happy are they who hope in the Lord.*

Luke 9:22-25 "If anyone wants to be a follower of mine..." (Luke 9:23).

In this Lenten season, Jesus calls us to follow him on the way that leads him to Jerusalem to be sacrificed on the Cross. "If any man would come after me, let him deny himself and take up his cross daily and follow me" (Lk 9:23). Of course, this is a demanding and difficult invitation, but it can unleash the creative power of love in those who accept it.

From the first moment of this season of Lent, therefore, our gaze is turned to Christ's glorious Cross. The author of the Imitation of Christ writes: "In the Cross is salvation; in the Cross is life; in the Cross is protection from the enemy; in the Cross is the supernatural gift of the sweetness of heaven; in the Cross is strength of mind and joy of spirit; in the Cross virtue is added to virtue and holiness is perfected" (XII, 1).

"Repent, and believe in the Gospel" (Mk 1:14). ...we listen again ...to this passage from the Evangelist Mark. It reminds us that the salvation offered by Jesus in his paschal mystery requires our response. Thus the liturgy urges us to give concrete and visible expression to the gift of conversion of heart, showing to us the way to take and the means to use. Attentive listening to God's Word, constant prayer, interior and exterior fasting, works of charity that concretely express our solidarity with our brothers and sisters: these matters cannot be avoided by those who, reborn to new life in Baptism, no longer intend to live according to the flesh but according to the Spirit (cf. Rom 8:4)."

Ash Wednesday Homily, February 12, 1997

Be diligent in handing on intact the spiritual heritage committed to you. Be faithful to your daily prayers, to the Holy Mass and the Sacrament of Penance, meeting regularly with Jesus as a loving and merciful Savior. Defend the sacredness of life and the holiness of Matrimony. Understand your holy Catholic faith and live by its teaching. Face up to the difficult challenges of modern life with Christian fortitude and patience. Did not Jesus himself say to his disciples: "If anyone wants to be a follower of mine, let him renounce himself and take up his cross and follow me" (Mt 16:24; Mk 8:34) *Homily, Glasgow, June 1, 1982*

To deny oneself is to give up one's own plans that are often small and petty in order to accept God's plan. This is the path of conversion, something indispensable in Christian life, and that led St. Paul to say, "it is no longer I who live, but Christ who lives in me" (Gal 2:20). Jesus does not ask us to give up living, but to accept a newness and a fullness of life that only He can give. The human being has a deep-rooted tendency to "think only of self", to regard one's own person as the centre of interest and to see oneself as the standard against which to gauge everything. One who chooses to follow Christ, on the other hand, avoids being wrapped up in himself and does not evaluate things according to self interest. He looks on life in terms of gift and gratuitousness, not in terms of conquest and possession. Life in its fullness is only lived in self-giving, and that is the fruit of the grace of Christ: an existence that is free and in communion with God and neighbour. *Message to Youth, February 14, 2001*

Friday after Ash Wednesday

Why fasting?

Readings of the day
Isaiah 58:1-9 *Is this not the sort of fast that pleases me?*
Psalm 50 *A broken, humbled heart, O God, you will not scorn.*

Matthew 9:14-15 "But the time will come for the bridegroom to be taken away from, and then they will fast" (Matthew 9:15).

Why fasting? At this moment there perhaps come into our minds the words with which Jesus answered the disciples of John the Baptist when they asked him: "Why do your disciples not fast?" Jesus answered: "Can the wedding guests mourn as long as the bridegroom is with them? The days will come, when the bridegroom is taken away from them, and then they will fast" (Mt 9:15). In fact the time of Lent reminds us that the bridegroom has been taken away from us. Taken away, arrested, imprisoned, slapped, scourged, crowned with thorns, crucified. ...Fasting in the time of Lent is the expression of our solidarity with Christ. Such was the meaning of Lent throughout the centuries and such it remains today…

Why fasting? It is necessary to give this question a wider and deeper answer, in order to clarify the relationship between fasting and "metanoia", that is, that spiritual change which brings man closer to God. …Man geared to material goods, multiple material goods, very often abuses them. It is not a question here just of food and drink. When man is geared exclusively to possession and use of material goods - that is, of things - then also the whole civilization is measured according to the quantity and the quality of the things with which it is in a position to supply man, and is not measured with the yardstick suitable for man. This civilization, in fact, supplies material goods not just in order that they may serve man to carry out creative and useful activities, but more and more... to satisfy the senses, the excitement he derives from them, momentary pleasure, an ever greater multiplicity of sensations…

It is seen from this that modern man must fast, that is, abstain not only from food or drink, but from many other means of consumption, stimulation, satisfaction of the senses. To fast: means to abstain, to renounce something.

Why renounce something? Why deprive oneself of it? We have already partly answered this question. However the answer will not be complete, if we do not realize that man is himself also because he succeeds in depriving himself of something, because he is capable of saying "no" to himself. Man is a being composed of body and soul. Some modern writers present this composite structure of man in the form of layers, and they speak, for example, of exterior layers on the surface of our personality, contrasting them with the layers in depth. Our life seems to be divided into such layers and takes place through them. While the superficial layers are bound up with our sensuality, the deep layers are an expression, on the contrary, of man's spirituality, that is, of conscious will, reflection, conscience, the capacity of living superior values. *General Audience, March 22, 1979*

Saturday after Ash Wednesday

Poverty in spirit and redemption

Readings of the day
Isaiah 58:9-14 *If you give what you have to feed the hungry, then your light will rise in the darkness.*
Psalm 85 *Teach me your way, O Lord, that I may be faithful in your sight.*

Luke 5:27-32 "And he left everything, and rose and followed him" (Luke 5:28).

The words and deeds of Jesus and those of his Church are not meant only for those who are sick or suffering or in some way neglected by society. On a deeper level they affect the very meaning of every person's life in its moral and spiritual dimensions. Only those who recognize that their life is marked by the evil of sin can discover in an encounter with Jesus the Savior the truth and the authenticity of their own existence. Jesus himself says as much: "Those who are well have no need of a physician, but those who are sick; I have not come to call the righteous, but sinners to repentance" (Lk 5.31-32).

But the person who, like the rich landowner in the Gospel parable, thinks that he can make his life secure by the possession of material goods alone, is deluding himself. Life is slipping away from him, and very soon he will find himself bereft of it without ever having appreciated its real meaning: "Fool! This night your soul is required of you; and the things you have prepared, whose will they be?" (Lk 12.20). *Evangelium vitae, 32*

Christ says: "Blessed are the poor in spirit" (Mt 5:3)…
Who are the poor in spirit? First of all, this has nothing to do with material poverty. According to Sacred Scripture, poverty in spirit concerns those who live with a supernatural vision. They live in the world, and they work and strive to earn their daily bread, but at the same time they are aware that all good

things come from God. Temporal goods, which they produce by the sweat of their brow, are also God's gift. The poor in spirit are those who attribute to themselves neither what they are nor what they possess. In fact, they recognize that they have received everything from God's hands, usually with the help of others. Thus they do not boast but praise the Lord for the good that they are able to achieve in their life and, in this way, they live in the truth. It could be said that the poor in spirit are precisely those who live in the truth and thereby become capable of accepting ever greater goods.

Jesus assures us that the poor in spirit possess the kingdom of heaven. In fact, the interior attitude of poverty ensures access to possession of the kingdom of heaven. In a certain sense it creates in man the interior space necessary to become a participant in the life and happiness of God.

The poor in spirit are the special objects of divine election… Poverty in spirit, according to the Gospel, indicates a sort of characteristic room man makes for God's action, allowing it to exercise its saving power. The kingdom of God is fulfilled in various ways when man opens the inner space of his soul to God, when he is not full of himself but open to the Fullness in an attitude of humility, so that in him God himself is praised. Then man lives on the truth of the Redemption, as we read in St. Paul's letter: "He is the source of your life in Christ Jesus, whom God made our wisdom, our righteousness and sanctification and redemption" (1 Cor 1:30). *Homily, January 28, 1996*

First Sunday of Lent

The hunger for God

Readings of the day
Genesis 2:7-9. 3:1-7 *The creation of our first parents, and their fall from grace through sin.*
Psalm 50 *Be merciful, O Lord, for we have sinned.*
Romans 5:12-19 *Where sin increased there grace abounded all the more.*

Matthew 4:1-11 "But he replied, 'Scripture says: Man does not live by bread alone'" (Matthew 4:4).

As followers of Christ, we do not despise the good things of the earth, for we know that these are created by God who is the source of all good. Nor do we try to ignore the need for bread, the great need for food suffered by so many throughout the world, even in our own lands. In fact, if we tried to ignore these basic needs of our brothers and sisters whom we can see, how could we claim to love God whom we cannot see (cf. 1 Jn 4:20)? And yet it remains true that "man does not live by bread alone". The human person has a need which is even deeper, a hunger which is even greater than bread can satisfy. It is the hunger of the human heart for the immensity of God. It is a hunger which can only be satisfied by him who said: "unless you eat the flesh of the Son of man and drink his blood, you have no life in you; he who eats my flesh and drinks my blood has eternal life, and I will raise him up at the last day. For my flesh is food indeed, and my blood is drink indeed" (Jn 6:53-55).

Christ is the only one who can satisfy the deepest hunger of the human heart. For he alone is the source of life. As Saint Paul wrote: "all things were created through him and for him. He is before all things, and in him all things hold together" (Col 1:16-17). In Christ, death has lost its power, death has been robbed of its sting, death has been defeated. This truth of our faith may seem paradoxical, since all around us we still see people frightened by the certainty of death and puzzled by the torment of pain. Indeed, pain and death weigh down the human spirit and remain an enigma for those who do not believe in God. But in faith we know that these will be overcome, that the victory has been won in the death and Resurrection of Jesus Christ, our Redeemer. And this is what we commemorate when we assemble in the name of the Most Holy Trinity; this is what we celebrate whenever we gather at the Eucharistic Sacrifice: we proclaim the death of the Lord until he comes in glory (cf. 1 Cor 11:26); we declare with one voice that Jesus Christ is the Lord - of the living and the dead, that he is the way and the truth and the life (cf. Jn 14:6), that Jesus Christ is the living bread which has been given for the life of the world (cf. Jn 6: 51). And it is the Eucharist which expresses our Savior's desire always to be present to each human heart, continually offering to each person a share in his life. What a wondrous gift is ours in the Eucharist! *Homily, Karachi, February 16, 1981*

The Church, expert teacher of humanity and holiness, shows us ancient and ever new instruments for the daily combat against evil suggestions: prayer, the sacraments, penance, careful attention to the Word of God, vigilance and fasting.

Let us undertake the penitential Lenten journey with greater determination, to be ready to defeat the seductions of Satan and arrive at Easter in joy of spirit. May Mary, Mother of Divine Mercy, be with us. *Homily, February 17, 2002*

Monday of the First Week of Lent

Conversion and the giving of alms

Readings of the day
Leviticus 19:1-2. 11-18 *Judge your neighbour justly.*
Psalm 18 *Your words, Lord, are spirit and life.*

Matthew 25:31-46 "For I was hungry and you gave me food" (Matthew 25:35).

"*Paenitemini et date eleemosynam*" (cf. Mk 1:15 and Lk 12:33).

Today we do not listen willingly to the word "alms". We feel something humiliating in it. This word seems to suppose a social system in which there reigns injustice, the unequal distribution of goods, a system which should be changed with adequate reforms. And if these reforms were not carried out, the need of radical changes, especially in the sphere of relations among men, would loom up on the horizon of social life. We find the same conviction in the texts of the Prophets of the Old Testament, on which the liturgy often draws during Lent. The Prophets consider this problem at the religious level: there is no true conversion to God, there can be no religion without putting right offences and injustices in relations among men, in social life. Yet in this context the Prophets exhort to alms deeds…

"Is not this the fast that I choose: to loose the bonds of wickedness, to undo the thongs of the yoke, / to let the oppressed go free, / and to break every yoke? / Is it not to share your bread with the hungry, / and bring the homeless poor into your house; / when you see the naked, to cover him, / and not to hide yourself from your own flesh?" (Is 58:6-7)…

Certainly Christ does not remove alms from our field of vision. He thinks also of pecuniary, material alms, but in his own way. More eloquent than any other, in this connection, is the example of the poor widow, who put a few small coins into the treasury of the Temple: from the material point of view, an offering that could hardly be compared with the offerings given by others. Yet Christ said: "This poor widow has put in… all the living that she had" (Lk 21:3-4). So it is, above all, the interior value of the gift that counts: the readiness to share everything, the readiness to give oneself.

Let us here recall St. Paul: "If I give away all I have… but have not love, I gain nothing" (1 Cor 13:3). St. Augustine, too, writes well in this connection: "if you stretch out your hand to give, but have not mercy in your heart, you have not done anything; but if you have mercy in your heart, even when you have nothing to give with your hand, God accepts your alms" (*Enarratio in Ps. CXXV, 5*).

We are here touching the heart of the problem. In Holy Scripture and according to the evangelical categories, "alms" means in the first place an interior gift. It means the attitude of opening "to the other". Precisely this attitude is an indispensable factor of "metanoia", that is, conversion, just as prayer and fasting are also indispensable. St. Augustine, in fact, expresses himself well: "how quickly the prayers of those who do good are granted! And this is man's justice in the present life: fasting, alms, prayer" (*Enarratio in Ps. XLII, 8*): prayer, as an opening to God; fasting, as an expression of self-mastery also in depriving oneself of something, in saying "no" to oneself; and finally alms, as opening "towards others". The Gospel draws this picture clearly when it speaks to us of repentance, of "metanoia". Only with a total attitude - in his relationship with God, with himself and with his neighbor - does man reach conversion and remain in the state of conversion." *General Audience, March 28, 1979*

Tuesday of the First Week of Lent

The foremost purpose of our prayer

Readings of the day
Isaiah 55:10-11 *My word carries out my will*
Psalm 33 *From all their afflictions God will deliver the just.*

Matthew 6:7-15 "And so we say: 'Our Father who art in heaven'" (Matthew 6:9).

When Jesus prays he uses the Aramaic word 'Abba' (cf. Mk 14:36), which is what small children would have called their fathers. Only Christ, the Eternal Son who is one in being with the Father, has the right to address with such familiarity, with such intimacy, the one whose throne is in the heavens. But we too have been given this privilege by our adoption as children of God in Baptism (cf. Rm 8:15; Gal 4:6). We have become sons and daughters 'in the Son' Jesus Christ. This unimagined and undeserved gift of communion with God transforms every human relationship. We pray not to 'my' father or to 'your' father, but to 'our Father'. Even when we "shut the door and pray... in secret" (Mt 6:6), we are spiritually united with all our brothers and sisters in Christ and with every human person created in the image and likeness of God and redeemed by the blood of the Lamb. Prayer delivers us from selfishness, from isolation and loneliness. It opens us up to the mystery of communion with God and with others.

"Hallowed be thy name. Thy kingdom come, thy will be done, on earth as it is in heaven" (Mt 6:9-10).

In the modern world, scientific and technological developments have dispelled many of our fears, relieved so many of the burdens of our existence, and opened up new possibilities for human self-realization. But these developments can also lead to a great temptation like the one "in the beginning" in the Book of Genesis: the temptation to decide for ourselves what is good and evil without reference to the God who made us, the vain attempt to place ourselves and our wills, rather than God and his law, at the center of the universe. But if we reject or ignore God "who is love", we reject love itself.

The first concern of the "Lord's Prayer" is that God's name should be glorified, that his Kingdom should come, that his will should be done. If that is our priority, then all else will be given us besides. Progress in science, economics, social organization and culture will not rob us of our humanity, but will reflect the love that alone gives life, meaning and body to our human efforts. It is God who "gives us our daily bread" (Mt 6: 11), even as we remember that it is not by bread alone that we live, "but by every word that proceeds from the mouth of God" (Mt 4:4). *Discourse, Trom (Norway), June 2, 1989*

Wednesday of the First Week of Lent

The greatest revelation of God and his mercy

Readings of the day
Jonah 3:1-10 *Nineveh was converted from its evil ways.*
Psalm 50 *A broken, humbled heart, O God, you will not scorn.*

Luke 11:29-32 "Something greater than Jonah is here" (Luke 11:32).

In John's Gospel we find a statement similar to that of the Letter to the Hebrews, but expressed more concisely. At the end of the Prologue we read: "No one has ever seen God; the only Son who is in the bosom of the Father, he has made him known" (Jn 1:18).

This is the essential difference between the revelation of God in the prophets and in the whole of the Old Testament, and that brought by Christ who says of himself: 'Behold, something greater than Jonah is here' (Mk 12 41). Here it is God himself, 'the Word made flesh' (cf. Jn 1:14) who speaks to us of God. That Word who 'is in the bosom of the Father' (Jn 1:18), becomes 'the true light' (Jn 1:9), 'the light of the world' (Jn 8:12). He says of himself, 'I am the way, the truth and the life' (Jn 14:6)…

If Christ's essential mission is to reveal the Father, who is 'our God' (cf. Jn 20:17), at the same time he himself is revealed by the Father as the Son. This Son, 'being one with the Father' (Jn 10:30), can therefore say: 'He who has seen me has seen the Father' (Jn 14:9). In Christ God has become 'visible'; God's 'visibility' is realized in Christ. St. Irenaeus expresses it concisely: 'The invisible Reality of the Son was the Father, and the visible Reality of the Father was the Son' (Adv. Haer. IV, 6, 6)…

"Let us return once again to the Second Vatican Council where we read: 'Jesus Christ… the Word made flesh, sent as a "man among men", "speaks the words of God" (Jn 3:34), and accomplishes the saving work which the Father gave him to do (cf. Jn 5:36; 17:4)'. He 'completed and perfected revelation and confirmed it with divine guarantees, by the very fact of his presence and self-manifestation, by words and works, signs and miracles, but above all by his death and glorious resurrection from the dead, and finally by sending the Spirit of truth. He revealed that God was with us, to deliver us from the darkness of sin and to raise us up to eternal life.

"'The Christian economy, therefore, since it is the new and definite covenant, will never pass away; and no new public revelation is to be expected before the glorious manifestation of our Lord Jesus Christ (cf. 1 Tim 6:14 and Tit 2:13)' (*Dei Verbum*, 4)" *General audience, June 1, 1988*

Thursday of the First Week of Lent

Trust and persevere in prayer

> ### *Readings of the day*
> **Esther 4:17** *I have no help other than you, Lord*
> **Psalm 137** *Lord, on the day I called for help, you answered me*
>
> **Matthew 7:7-12 "Ask, and it will be given to you; search, and you will find; knock, and the door will be opened to you" (Matthew 7:7).**

"Lord, teach us to pray…" (Lk 11:1), one of his disciples says to Christ in the Gospel. And he answers them referring to the example of a man, yes, an importunate man, who, finding himself in need, knocks at his friend's door at midnight. But he obtains what he asks for. Jesus, therefore, encourages us to have a similar attitude in prayer: that of ardent perseverance. He says: "Ask, and it will be given you; seek, and you will find; knock, and it will be opened to you…" (Mt 7:7).

"A model of such persevering prayer, humble and, at the same time, confident, is found in the Old Testament, in Abraham, who beseeches God for the salvation of Sodom and Gomorrah, if there were at last ten righteous men to be found there.

"In this way, therefore, we must encourage ourselves more and more to prayer. We must often remember Christ's exhortation: "Ask, and it will be given you; seek, and you will find; knock, and it will be opened to you." In particular, we must remember it when we lose confidence or the desire to pray.

"We must also learn anew to pray, always. It often happens that we dispense ourselves from praying with the excuse that we are unable to do so. If we really do not know how to pray, then it is all the more necessary; to learn. That is important for everyone, and it seems to be particularly important for the young, who often neglect the prayer they learned as children, because it seems to them too childish, naive, and superficial. Such a state of mind is, on the contrary, an indirect incentive to deepen one's prayer, to make it more thoughtful, more mature, to seek support for it in the Word of God himself and in the Holy Spirit, who "intercedes for us with sighs too deep for words", as St. Paul writes (Rom 8:26)." *Angelus message, July 27, 1980*

We know well that prayer cannot be taken for granted. We have to learn to pray: as it were learning this art ever anew from the lips of the Divine Master himself, like the first disciples: "Lord, teach us to pray!" (Lk 11:1). Prayer develops that conversation with Christ which makes us his intimate friends: "Abide in me and I in you" (Jn 15:4). This reciprocity is the very substance and soul of the Christian life… Wrought in us by the Holy Spirit, this reciprocity opens us, through Christ and in Christ, to contemplation of the Father's face. Learning this Trinitarian shape of Christian prayer and living it fully, above all in the liturgy, the summit and source of the Church's life, but also in personal experience, is the secret of a truly vital Christianity, which has no reason to fear the future, because it returns continually to the sources and finds in them new life…

Yes, dear brothers and sisters, our Christian communities must become genuine 'schools' of prayer, where the meeting with Christ is expressed not just in imploring help but also in thanksgiving, praise, adoration, contemplation, listening and ardent devotion, until the heart truly "falls in love". Intense prayer, yes, but it does distract us from our commitment to history: by opening our heart to the love of God it also opens it to the love of our brothers and sisters, and makes us capable of shaping history according to God's plan. *Novo millennio ineunte, January 6, 2001*

Friday of the First Week of Lent

Forgive and we will be forgiven

Readings of the day

Ezekiel 18:21-28 *If the wicked turn away from their sins, they shall live.*

Psalm 129 *If you, O Lord, laid bare our guilt, who could endure it?*

Matthew 5:20-26 "But I say to you that every one who is angry with his brother shall be liable to judgement" (Matthew 5:22).

The commandment "You shall not kill," included and more fully expressed in the positive command of love for one's neighbor, is reaffirmed in all its force by the Lord Jesus. To the rich young man who asks him: "Teacher, what good deed must I do, to have eternal life?," Jesus replies: "If you would enter life, keep the commandments" (Mt 19.16, 17). And he quotes, as the first of these: "You shall not kill" (Mt 19.18). In the Sermon on the Mount, Jesus demands from his disciples a righteousness which surpasses that of the Scribes and Pharisees, also with regard to respect for life: "You have heard that it was said to the men of old, 'You shall not kill;' and 'whoever kills shall be liable to judgment.' But I say to you that every one who is angry with his brother shall be liable to judgment" (Mt 5.21-22).

By his words and actions Jesus further unveils the positive requirements of the commandment regarding the inviolability of life. These requirements were already present in the Old Testament, where legislation dealt with protecting and defending life when it was weak and threatened: in the case of foreigners, widows, orphans, the sick and the poor in general, including children in the womb (cf. Ex 21.22; 22.20-26). With Jesus, these positive requirements assume new force and urgency, and are revealed in all their breadth and depth: they range from caring for the life of one's brother (whether a blood brother, someone belonging to the same people, or a foreigner living in the land of Israel) to showing concern for the stranger, even to the point of loving one's enemy.

A stranger is no longer a stranger for the person who must become a neighbor to someone in need, to the point of accepting responsibility for his life, as the parable of the Good Samaritan shows so clearly (cf. Lk 10.25-37). Even an enemy ceases to be an enemy for the person who is obliged to love him (cf. Mt 5.38-48; Lk 6.27-35), to 'do good' to him (cf. Lk 6.27, 33, 35) and to respond to his immediate needs promptly and with no expectation of repayment (cf. Lk 6.34-35). The height of this love is to pray for one's enemy. By so doing we achieve harmony with the providential love of God: "But I say to you, love your enemies and pray for those who persecute you, so that you may be children of your Father who is in heaven; for he makes his sun rise on the evil and on the good and sends rain on the just and on the unjust" (Mt 5.44-45; cf. Lk 6.28,35).

Thus the deepest element of God's commandment to protect human life is the requirement to show reverence and love for every person and the life of every person. This is the teaching which the Apostle Paul, echoing the words of Jesus, addresses to the Christians in Rome: "The commandments, 'You shall not commit adultery, You shall not kill, You shall not steal, You shall not covet,' and any other commandment, are summed up in this sentence, 'You shall love your neighbor as yourself.'" "Love does no wrong to a neighbor; therefore love is the fulfilling of the law" (Rom 13.9-10). *Evangelium vitae, 41*

Saturday of the First Week of Lent

Everyone is called to holiness

> #### *Readings of the day*
> **Deuteronomy 26:16-19** *You will be a people consecrated to the Lord*
> **Psalm 118** *Happy are they who follow the Lord!*
>
> **Matthew 5:43-48 "Be perfect as your heavenly Father is perfect" (Matthew 5:48).**

The Church is holy and all her members are called to holiness. Lay people participate in the Church's holiness as fully qualified members of the Christian community: this participation, which we could call ontological, also becomes for lay people a personal ethical commitment to sanctification. In this capacity and in this vocation to holiness, all the members of the Church are equal (cf. Gal 3:28). The degree of personal holiness does not depend on the position occurred in society or in the Church, but does rely on the degree to which charity is lived (cf. 1 Cor 13). A lay person who generously welcomes divine charity in his heart and in his life is holier than a priest or Bishop who accepts it half-heartedly…

The Council asserts: "The followers of Christ, called by God not in virtue of their works but by his design and grace, and justified in the Lord Jesus, have been made children of God in the baptism of faith and partakers of the divine nature, and so are truly sanctified" (Lumen Gentium n. 40). Holiness means belonging to God; this belonging is realized in Baptism, when Christ takes possession of the human being, to make him "share in the divine nature" (cf. 2 Pt 1:4) which is in him by virtue of the Incarnation (cf. Summa Theol, III, q. 7, a. 13; q. 8, a. 5). Thus Christ truly becomes, as has been said, "the life of the soul". The sacramental character imprinted on the person by Baptism is the sign and the bond of consecration to God. This is why Paul, speaking of the baptized, calls them 'saints' (cf. Rom 1:7; 1 Cor 1:2; 2 Cor 1:1, etc.)…

All must strive for holiness, because they already possess the seed in themselves; they must nurture this holiness which has been given them. Everyone must live "as is fitting among saints" (Eph 5:3), and put on, "as God's chosen ones, holy and beloved, heartfelt compassion, kindness, humility, gentleness and patience" (Col 3:12). In the baptized, the holiness that they possess shields them neither from temptation nor from every fault, because the weakness of human nature persists in this life…

To strive for perfection is not the privilege of some, but an obligation for all the members of the Church. The commitment to Christian perfection means persevering on the way of holiness. As the Council states: "The Lord Jesus, divine teacher and model of perfection, preached holiness of life (of which he is the author and maker) to each and every one of his disciples without distinction: 'You therefore, must be perfect, as your heavenly Father is perfect'" (Mt 5:48), (*Lumen Gentium*, n. 40). Therefore, "All Christians in any state or walk of life are called to the fullness of Christian life and to the perfection of love" (ibid.). Precisely through the sanctification of each person, a new human perfection is introduced in earthly society (ibid.). In the words of the Servant of God, Elizabeth Leseur, "Every soul that rises raises the world with it". The Council teaches that "from this holiness a more human manner of life is fostered even in earthly society" (ibid.). *General Audience, November 24, 1993*

Second Sunday of Lent

True apostolate requires personal relationship with Christ

Readings of the day

Genesis 12:1-4 *The call of Abraham, the father of God's people.*

Psalm 32 *Lord, let your mercy be on us, as we place our trust in you.*

2 Timothy 1:8-10 *God has saved us, and called us to be holy.*

Matthew 17:1-9 "This is my beloved Son, with whom I am well pleased. Listen to him" (Matthew 17:5).

"This is my beloved Son, with whom I am well pleased" (Mt 17:5) The Father's invitation to the disciples who were privileged witnesses of the extraordinary event of the Transfiguration still echoes today for us and for all the Church. Like Peter, James and John, we too are invited to climb Mount Tabor with Jesus and to let ourselves be awed by the splendour of his glory. On this Second Sunday of Lent, we contemplate Christ enveloped in light, in the company of Moses and Elijah, authoritative spokesmen of the Old Testament. To him we renew our personal adherence: he is the Father's "beloved Son."

Listen to him! This pressing appeal spurs us to intensify our Lenten journey. It is an invitation to let the light of Christ illuminate our life and give us the strength to proclaim and bear witness to the Gospel to our brothers and sisters. It is a task, as we know well, which sometimes means hardship and suffering. This is also stressed by St. Paul, who says to his faithful disciple Timothy: *"Take your share of suffering for the Gospel"* (2 Tm 1:8).

The experience of Jesus' Transfiguration prepares the Apostles to face the tragic events of Calvary by showing them in advance what will be the full and definitive revelation of the Master's glory in the paschal mystery. Meditating on this Gospel passage, we too are preparing to relive the decisive events of the Lord's Death and Resurrection, following him on the way of the Cross to attain light and glory. Indeed, we must first "suffer and so come to the glory of his Resurrection" *(Preface)*…

In this important season of Lent …I once again urge you to approach with trust [the] sacrament of spiritual healing. It makes sacramentally present Jesus' call to conversion and the path that leads us back to the Father, from whom man distances himself through sin…

For the sacrament of Penance to be truly celebrated, it is necessary that the confession of sins arise from serious and careful reflection on the Word of God and living contact with the person of Christ. For this purpose, an appropriate catechesis is needed… which aims at putting people in communion with Jesus, for only he can lead us to the love of the Father in the Holy Spirit and make us share in the life of the Holy Trinity…

Is it not precisely from knowing Christ, his person, his love and his truth that those who experience him personally feel an irresistible desire to proclaim him to everyone, to evangelise and to lead others to the discovery of the faith? I sincerely hope that each of you will be more and more inspired by this longing for Christ, the source of genuine missionary spirit…

Blessed Virgin, Star of evangelisation, help us to understand your Son's words and to proclaim them generously and consistently to our brethren. *Homily, Ostia, February 28, 1999*

Monday of the Second Week of Lent

God is our Father and he forgives

> *Readings of the day*
> **Daniel 9:4-10** *We have sinned, we have done wrong.*
> **Psalm 78** *Lord, do not deal with us as our sins deserve.*
>
> **Luke 6:36-38** **"Be compassionate as your heavenly Father is compassionate" (Luke 6:36).**

[The] fatherhood [of God] regards not only the chosen people, but reaches every man and surpasses the bond existing with earthly parents. Here are some texts: "For my father and mother have forsaken me, but the Lord will take me up" (Ps 26 [27] : 10). "As a father pities his children, so the Lord pities those who fear him" (Ps 102 [103]:13). "The Lord reproves him whom he loves, as a father the son in whom he delights" (Prov 3:12). In the texts just quoted there is evident the analogical character of the fatherhood of God the Lord to whom there is directed the prayer: "O Lord, Father and Ruler of my life, do not abandon me to their counsel, and let me not fall because of them… O Lord, Father and God of my life, do not leave me at the mercy of brazen looks" (Sir 23:1-4). In the same light he again says: "If the righteous man is God's son, he will help him, and will deliver him from the hand of his adversaries" (Wis 2:18). God's fatherhood, both in regard to Israel and to individuals is manifested in merciful love. We read, for example, in Jeremiah: "With weeping they had departed, and with consolations I will lead them back… for I am a father to Israel, and Ephraim is my firstborn" (Jer 31:9). There are numerous passages in the Old Testament which present the merciful love of the God of the Covenant. Here are some of them: "But thou art merciful to all, for thou canst do all things, and thou dost overlook men's sin, that they may repent… Thou sparest all things, for they are thine, O Lord who lovest the living" (Wis 11:23-26).

"I have loved you with an everlasting love; therefore I have continued my faithfulness to you" (Jer 31:3).

In Isaiah we meet moving testimonies of care and affection: "But Zion said, 'The Lord has forsaken me, my Lord has forgotten me'. Can a woman forget her sucking child? Even if she forget, yet I will not forget you" (Is 49:14-15; cf. also 54:10).

It is significant that in the passages of the prophet Isaiah God's fatherhood is enriched with allusions inspired by motherhood (cf. Dives in Misericordia, note 52). In the fullness of the Messianic times Jesus frequently announces God's fatherhood in regard to mankind by linking it with the numerous expressions contained in the Old Testament. Thus it is expressed concerning Divine Providence in regard to creatures, especially in regard to man: "…your heavenly Father feeds them…" (Mt 6:26; cf. Lk 12:24); "Your heavenly Father knows that you need them all" (Mt 6:32; cf. Lk 12:30). Jesus seeks to make the divine mercy understood by presenting as proper to God the welcoming reception of the father for the prodigal son (cf. Lk 15:11-32); and he exhorts those who hear his word: Be merciful, even as your Father is merciful" (Lk 6:36).

To conclude, we can say that, through Jesus, God is not only "the Father of Israel, the Father of mankind", but "our Father". *General audience, October 16, 1985*

Tuesday of the Second Week of Lent

Serve so as to reign

Readings of the day
Isaiah 1:10. 16-20 *Learn to do good, search for justice.*
Psalm 49 *To the upright I will show the saving power of God.*

Matthew 23:1-12 "The greatest among you must be your servant" (Matthew 23:1-12).

Have you not perhaps come here - I ask you again - to convince yourselves once and for all that to be great means to serve? This service is certainly not mere humanitarian sentimentality. Nor is the community of the disciples of Christ a volunteer agency or social help group. Such a concept of service would imply stooping to the level of the "spirit of this world." No! Here we are dealing with something more. The radicality, quality and destiny of this 'service' to which we have all been called must be seen in the context of the human Redemption. Because we have been created, we have been called, we have been destined, first and foremost, to serve God, in the image and likeness of Christ who, as Lord of all creation, as center of the cosmos and of history, showed his royal power through obedience unto death, and was glorified in the Resurrection (*cf. Lumen Gentium*, 36). The kingdom of God is realized by means of this service which is the fullness and measure of all human service. It does not act, according to human criteria, through power, might and money. Each one of us is asked for a total readiness to follow Christ, who "came not to be served, but to serve."

To serve; to be a person for others.

This is also a truth which the Apostle Paul teaches very eloquently…

"I bid every one among you not to think of himself more

highly than he ought to think, but to think with sober judgment, each according to the measure of faith which God has assigned to him" (Rom 12:3).

And the Apostle adds: "Having gifts that differ" (Rom 12:6).

Yes! You need to know well the gifts God has granted you in Christ. It is necessary to know well the gift you have received, in order to give it to others, to contribute to the common good.

Yes. You need to perceive well the gifts God has granted you in Christ. You need to know well the gift you have received in the very experience of family and parish life, in working together with others in associations, and in the charismatic flourishing of movements, so as to be able to give it to others: thus to enrich the communion and missionary thrust of the Church, to be witnesses of Christ in your neighborhood and school, in the university and factory, in places of work and recreation, …to contribute to the common good, as servants of experiences of growth in humanity, of dignity and solidarity… This is what the apostle teaches. What he says is not just a mere teaching, but a fervent call. "Let love be genuine; hate what is evil, hold fast to what is good; love one another with brotherly affection; outdo one another in showing honor. Never flag in zeal, be aglow with the spirit, serve the Lord. Rejoice in your hope, be patient in tribulation, be constant in prayer. Contribute to the needs of the saints, practice hospitality" (Rom 12:9 - 13) *Homily, Santiago de Compostela, August 20, 1989*

Wednesday of the Second Week of Lent

Be ready to suffer and sacrifice for Christ

Readings of the day
Jeremiah 18:18-20 *Come, let us persecute him.*
Psalm 30 *Save me, O Lord, in your steadfast love.*

Matthew 20:17-28 "'Can you drink the cup that I am going to drink?' They replied, 'We can'" (Matthew 20:22).

Look at James, son of Zebedee, a fisherman like his father and brother; the son of a determined mother. James followed Jesus of Nazareth. When, in reply to their mother's question the Master asked, "Are you able to drink the cup that I am to drink?" (Mt 20:22), James and his brother John answered without a doubt: "We are able" (Mt 20:22).

This is not a calculated reply, but rather one which is full of confidence.

James did not yet know, and in any case if he knew something, he did not fully know, what this "cup" meant. Christ was speaking of the cup which he himself had to drink, the cup which he had received from the Father.

The moment came when Christ fulfilled what he had earlier announced. He drank the cup, which his Father had given him, to the last drop.

The truth is that James was not with his Master on Golgotha. Neither were Peter nor the other Apostles. Only John remained with Christ's Mother - he alone. Nevertheless, later all of them understood - and James understood - the truth about the 'cup.' He understood that Christ had to drink it to the last drop. He understood that it was necessary for him to undergo all that; that he had to suffer death on a cross . . .

Christ, in effect, the Son of God, came "not to be served, but to serve and to give his life as a ransom for many" (Mt 20:28).

Christ is the servant of human Redemption!…

However …are you prepared to drink of this cup? Are you prepared to let yourselves be permeated by the body and blood of Christ, so as to die to the old man which is in us and rise again with him? Do you feel the Lord's strength which can enable you to bear your sacrifices, sufferings and the 'cross' which weigh upon [those] who are disoriented as regards the meaning of life, manipulated by power, unemployed, hungry, submerged in drugs and violence, slaves of the eroticism which is spreading everywhere? …Know that Christ's yoke is easy… and that only in him will we find the hundred fold here and now, and eternal life later…

I invite you, dear friends, to discover your true vocation to cooperate in the spreading of this Kingdom of truth and life, of holiness and grace, of justice, love and peace. If you really wish to serve your brothers and sisters, let Christ reign in your hearts, let him help you to discern and grow in dominion over yourselves, strengthen you in the virtues, to fill you above all with his charity, to guide you along the path which leads to the "condition of the perfect one." Do not be afraid to be saints! *Homily, Santiago de Compostela, October 16, 1994*

Thursday of the Second Week of Lent

Social justice calls for a conversion

Readings of the day

Jeremiah 17:5-10 *A curse on those who trust in humanity; a blessing on those who trust in the Lord God.*
Psalm 1 *Happy are they who hope in the Lord.*

Luke 16:19-31 "If they will not listen to Moses or to the prophets, they will not be convinced even if someone should rise from the dead" (Luke 16:31).

Man's situation today is certainly not uniform but marked with numerous differences. These differences have causes in history, but they also have strong ethical effects. Indeed everyone is familiar with the picture of the consumer civilization, which consists in a certain surplus of goods necessary for man and for entire societies - and we are dealing precisely with the rich, highly developed societies - while the remaining societies - at least broad sectors of them - are suffering from hunger, with many people dying each day of starvation and malnutrition. Hand in hand go a certain abuse of freedom by one group - an abuse linked precisely with a consumer attitude uncontrolled by ethics - and a limitation by it of the freedom of the others, that is to say, those suffering marked shortages and being driven to conditions of even worse misery and destitution.

This pattern, which is familiar to all, and the contrast referred to, …represent, as it were, the gigantic development of the parable in the Bible of the rich banqueter and the poor man Lazarus. So widespread is the phenomenon that it brings into question the financial, monetary, production and commercial mechanisms that, resting on various political pressures, support the world economy. These are proving incapable either of remedying the unjust social situations inherited from the past or of dealing with the urgent challenges and ethical demands of the present. By submitting man to tensions created by him-self, dilapidating at an accelerated pace material and energy resources, and compromising the geophysical environment, these structures unceasingly make the areas of misery spread, accompanied by anguish, frustration and bitterness.

We have before us here a great drama that can leave nobody indifferent. The person who, on the one hand, is trying to draw the maximum profit and, on the other hand, is paying the price in damage and injury is always man. The drama is made still worse by the presence close at hand of the privileged social classes and of the rich countries, which accumulate goods to an excessive degree and the misuse of whose riches very often becomes the cause of various ills. Add to this the fever of infla-tion and the plague of unemployment - these are further symp-toms of the moral disorder that is being noticed in the world situation and therefore requires daring creative resolves in keeping with man's authentic dignity… This difficult road of the indispensable transformation of the structures of economic life is one on which it will not be easy to go forward without the intervention of a true conversion of mind, will and heart. The task requires resolute commitment by individuals and peoples that are free and linked in solidarity. *Redemptor hominis, 16*

Friday of the Second Week of Lent

Jesus' suffering is God's love for us

Readings of the day
Genesis 37:3-4. 12-13. 17-28 *Here comes the man of dreams; let us kill him.*
Psalm 104 *Remember the marvels the Lord has done.*

Matthew 21:33-43. 45-46 "…they seized him and threw him out of the vineyard and killed him'
(Matthew 21:39).

If the truth about Jesus Christ as the Son sent by the Father is set out clearly especially in the Johannine texts, it is however also contained in the Synoptic Gospels. There we see, for example, that Jesus said, "I must preach the kingdom to the other cities also; for I was sent for this purpose" (Lk 4:43). Of particular importance is the parable of the wicked tenant farmers. They treated badly the servants, sent by the owner of the vineyard "to get from them some of the fruit of the vineyard" (Mk 12: 2), and they killed many of them. Finally, the owner of the vineyard decided to send to them his own son, "He had still one other, a beloved son; finally he sent him to them, saying, 'They will respect my son!' But those tenants said to one another, 'This is the heir; come, let us kill him, and the inheritance will be ours.' And they took him and killed him, and cast him out of the vineyard" (Mk 12:6-8). Commenting on this parable, Jesus recalls what was written in Psalm 117/118 about the stone rejected by the builders: it was this very stone that became the head of the corner (that is, the cornerstone) (cf. Ps 117/118:22).

The parable of the son sent to the tenants of the vineyard is recorded by all the Synoptics (cf. Mk 12:1-12; Mt 21:33-46; Lk 20:9-19). From it clearly emerges the truth about Jesus sent by the Father. Indeed, it emphasizes rather graphically the sacrificial and redemptive character of the mission. The Son is truly "he whom the Father consecrated and sent into the world" (Jn 10:36). Thus, God not only "spoke to us by a Son... in these last days" (cf. Heb 1:1-2), but he has given for us this Son, in an act of incomprehensible love, by sending him into the world.

In these terms John's Gospel also speaks in a particularly moving way, "For God so loved the world that he gave his only Son, that whoever believes in him should not perish but have eternal life" (Jn 3:16). And he adds, "God sent his only Son into the world, as the saviour of the world" (v.17). Elsewhere John writes, "God is love… In this the love of God was made manifest among us, that God sent his only Son into the world, so that we might live through him. In this is love, not that we loved God but that he loved us and sent his Son to be the expiation for our sins" (1 John 4:7-10). Therefore he adds that in accepting Jesus, his Gospel, his death and resurrection, "we know and believe the love God has for us. God is love, and he who abides in love abides in God, and God abides in him" (cf. 1 Jn 4:16). *General audience, June 27, 1984*

The Son has become "the first-born among many brethren" (Rom 8:29); through his death the Father communicated new life to us (1 Pt 1:3; cf also Rom 8:32; Eph 1:3), so that we might call upon him in the Holy Spirit with the same term that Jesus used: Abba (Rom 8:15; Gal 4:6). St. Paul explains this mystery further saying that "the Father …has qualified us to share in the inheritance of the saints in light. He has delivered us from the dominion of darkness and transferred us to the kingdom of his beloved Son" (Col 1:12-13). *General audience, March 10, 1999*

Saturday of the Second Week of Lent

God always wants our reconciliation

Readings of the day
Micah 7:14-15. 18-20 *You will cast all our sins into the depths of the sea.*
Psalm 102 *The Lord is kind and merciful.*

Luke 15:1-3. 11-32 "While he was still a long way off, his father saw him and was moved with pity" (Luke 15:20).

This prodigal son is man every human being: bewitched by the temptation to separate himself from his Father in order to lead his own independent existence; disappointed by the emptiness of the mirage which had fascinated him: alone, dishonored, exploited when he tries to build a world all for himself; sorely tried, even in the depths of his own misery, by the desire to return to communion with his Father. Like the father in the parable, God looks out for the return of his child, embraces him when he arrives and orders the banquet of the new meeting with which the reconciliation is celebrated.

The most striking element of the parable is the father's festive and loving welcome of the returning son: it is a sign of the mercy of God, who is always willing to forgive. Let us say at once: reconciliation is principally a gift of the heavenly Father.

But the parable also brings into the picture the elder brother, who refuses to take his place at the banquet. He rebukes his younger brother for his dissolute wanderings, and he rebukes his father for the welcome given to the prodigal son while he himself, a temperate and hard-working person, faithful to father and home, has never been allowed, he says, to have a celebration with his friends. This is a sign that he does not understand the father's goodness. To the extent that this brother, too sure of himself and his own good qualities, jealous and haughty, full of bitterness and anger, is not converted and is not reconciled with his father and brother, the banquet is not yet fully the celebration of a reunion and rediscovery.

Man - every human being - is also this elder brother. Selfishness makes him jealous, hardens his heart, blinds him and shuts him off from other people and from God. The loving kindness and mercy of the father irritate and enrage him; for him the happiness of the brother who has been found again has a bitter taste. From this point of view he too needs to be converted in order to be reconciled. *Reconciliatio et paenitentia*, 5,6

The father of today's parable loves without conditions and without limitations. He is not a father who exploits his son or who humiliates him or who uses him or who prevents him from growing, as unfortunately, can happen on this earth through human frailty. The heavenly Father, while being aware of the sins, the limitations and the defects of his children, loves them just as they are. And when they return to him, even if for selfish reasons like those of the prodigal son, who thought of himself and not of his father, he welcomes them with great joy, ordering that they should wear the most beautiful robes, a ring on their finger, sandals on their feet and that a festive banquet should be prepared. Only the one whose heart is hardened through sin, who is blinded by selfishness and by dissolute passions, can offer resistance to his love and can persevere in obstinacy and in evil, refusing to begin that process of conversion which is necessary for the one who truly desires to meet the Father. For this reason let us listen to the cry of St. Paul: "We implore you on behalf of Christ, be reconciled to God" (2 Cor 5:20). *Homily, March 29, 1992*

Third Sunday of Lent

The Holy Spirit, holiness and confession

Readings of the day
Exodus 17:3-7 *Give us water to drink.*
Psalm 94 *If today you hear his voice, harden not your hearts.*
Romans 5:1-2. 5-8 *The love of God has been poured into our hearts by the Holy Spirit which has been given to us.*

John 4:5-42 "He told me all that I have ever done" (John 4:39).

The Samaritan woman is surprised by these words. What is the living water? Jesus himself explains: "Whoever drinks of the water that I shall give him will never thirst; the water that I shall give him will become in him a spring of water welling up to eternal life" (Jn 4:14). He speaks of "living water", that is, of the love of God poured into our hearts by the Holy Spirit. Divine love becomes in man the spring of eternal life, capable of satisfying all his deepest desires, temporal, but first and foremost, those eternal…

The Spirit lives in baptized persons as in a temple. Therefore, every Christian is called to be holy, like his heavenly Father. This truth, so clearly proclaimed by Jesus in the Gospel, was witnessed to by Blessed Josemaria Escriva through his life and constant teaching. "God awaits us every day", he loved to repeat. "Be sure of this: there is something holy, divine, hidden in the most ordinary situations, something that each one of us must discover". And he used to add: "There is no other way, my children: either we know how to find the Lord in our ordinary lives, or we will never find him" *(Conversations with Mons. Escriva de Balaguer, n. 114)*.

Dear brothers and sisters, may you know how to make your own his program of life and pastoral commitment: to live by striving for holiness and to let every person you meet, whether man or woman, understand that they are called to full communion with God… We are well aware that dialogue with souls, if carried out in a profound manner, develops slowly. Do not abandon this fundamental apostolate; the concrete fruits, even though slow in coming, will certainly not fail to arrive.

The conversation with the Samaritan woman, which we heard in today's Gospel, speaks indirectly about the Holy Spirit as "the light of hearts". The woman in fact admits that Christ knows her sins even before she had confided them to him; in this way she sees that he is a prophet. This is a particularly significant theme during the Lenten season. The "light of the heart" is necessary for a good preparation for the celebration of Easter, including through the sacrament of Penance.

Especially during Lent, all the faithful are invited to study more deeply the value of Confession as a fundamental moment for recognizing the evil and sin that are present in their lives, for being reconciled with God and with their brothers, and for renewing their loyalty to Christ and his Gospel…

Light of the Holy Spirit, illumine our lives, help us to be generously involved in this season of Lent, proclaim to us, even now, the splendor of the light and joy of Easter.

Lord, you are truly the Savior of the world; give us the living water, so that we will no longer thirst for all eternity (cf. Gospel acclamation). Amen! *Homily, March 10, 1996*

Monday of the Third Week of Lent

Spirit of poverty opens to spiritual riches

Readings of the day
Kings 5:1-15 *There were many lepers in Israel, but none were made clean, except Naaman the Syrian.*
Psalm 41 *My soul is thirsting for the living God: when shall I see him face to face.*

Luke 4:24-30 "Elijah… was sent to a widow at Zarephath, a Sidonian town" (Luke 4:26).

To reach the Father's house we must let ourselves be guided by the truth, which Jesus expressed in his life and his teaching. It is a rich and universal truth. It reveals to the eyes of our soul the vast horizons of the great works of God. And, at the same time, it penetrates so deeply into the mysteries of the human heart, as only the divine Word can do. The liturgy of today seems to recall to us, with a particular accent, one of the elements of this truth.

"Blessed are the poor in spirit for theirs is the kingdom of heaven" (Mt 5:3). It can be said that the liturgy… illustrates in a particularly inspiring way this first beatitude of the Sermon on the Mount, permitting us to penetrate thoroughly the truth it contains. In the first reading, we hear of the poor widow of the time of Elijah, who lived at Zarephath, in Sidon. …[She] gave Elijah her last handful of flour to make a little cake. …[She] does not remain disappointed because, in accordance with Elijah's prophecy, "The jar of meal was not spent until the day that the Lord sent rain upon the earth" (cf. 1 Kings 17:14)…

It may sound like a paradox, but this poverty conceals within itself special riches. The rich man, in fact, is not he who has, but he who gives. He gives not so much what he possesses, as himself. Then he can give even when he does not possess. So even when he does not possess, he is rich.

Man is poor, on the contrary, not because he does not possess, but because he is bound - and particularly when he is bound spasmodically and completely - to what he possesses. When he is bound in such a way that he is not able to give anything. When he is not able to be open to others and give himself to them. In the rich man's heart all the goods of this world become dead. In the poor man's heart, in the sense of which I am speaking, even the smallest goods come to life again and become great.

Certainly, the world has changed a great deal since Christ uttered the beatitude of the poor in spirit, in the Sermon on the Mount. The times in which we live are quite different from those of Christ. We are living in another era of history, civilization, technology and economy. Yet Christ's words have not lost anything of their accuracy, their depth, their truth. On the contrary, they have acquired a new significance....

As at the time of the Sermon on the Mount, so today, too, each of us must judge, by the truth of Christ's words, his works and his heart. *Homily, November 11, 1979*

Tuesday of the Third Week of Lent

Set no limits on your forgiveness

Readings of the day
Daniel 3:25. 34-43 *We ask you to receive us with humble and contrite hearts.*
Psalm 24 *Remember your mercies, Lord.*

Matthew 18:21-35 "Not seven, I tell you, but seventy-seven times" (Matthew 18:22).

Peter asks Jesus the questions:
"Lord, how often shall my brother sin against me, and I forgive him? As many as seven times?" Jesus said to him, "I do not say to you seven times, but seventy times seven" (Mt 18:21-22).

"Seventy times seven": with this reply the Lord wants to make it clear to Peter and to us that we should set no limit to our forgiveness of others. Just as the Lord is always ready to forgive us, so we must always be ready to forgive one another. And how great is the need for forgiveness and reconciliation in our world today; indeed in our communities and families, in our very own hearts! That is why the special sacrament of the Church for forgiveness, the Sacrament of Penance, is such a precious gift from the Lord.

In the Sacrament of Penance, God extends his forgiveness to us in a very personal way. Through the ministry of the priest, we come to our loving Savior with the burden of our sins. We confess that we have sinned against God and our neighbor. We manifest our sorrow and ask for pardon from the Lord. Then, through the priest, we hear Christ say to us: "Your sins are forgiven" (Mk 2:5); "Go, and do not sin again" (Jn 8:11). Can we not also hear him say to us as we are filled with his saving grace: "Extend to others, seventy times seven, this same forgiveness and mercy?"

This is the work of the Church in every age - it is the duty of each one of us "to profess and proclaim God's mercy in all its truth" (Dives in Misericordia, 13), to extend to whomever we meet each day the same unlimited forgiveness that we have received from Christ. We practice mercy, too, when we "bear with one another charitably, in complete selflessness, gentleness and patience" (Eph 4:2). And God's mercy is also shown by generous and untiring service, like that required in offering health care for the sick or in carrying out medical research with persevering dedication …let us praise our God who is rich in mercy. And, in imitation of his great love, let us forgive anyone who may have hurt us in any way. *Angelus September 16, 1984*

Surely this is one of the most difficult and radical commands of the Gospel. Yet how much suffering and anguish, how much futility, destruction and violence would be avoided, if only we put into practice in all our human relationships the Lord's answer to Peter.

Merciful love is absolutely necessary, in particular, for people who are close to one another: for husbands and wives, parents and children, and among friends (cf. Dives in Misericordia, 14) At a time when family life is under such great stress, when a high number of divorces and broken homes are a sad fact of life, we must ask ourselves whether human relationships are being based, as they should be, on the merciful love and forgiveness revealed by God in Jesus Christ. We must examine our own heart and see how willing we are to forgive and to accept forgiveness in this world as well as in the next. *Homily, New Orleans, September 12, 1987*

Wednesday of the Third Week of Lent

Live by the commandments to live forever

Readings of the day
Deuteronomy 4:1. 5-9 *Keep the commandments and your work will be complete.*
Psalm 147 *Praise the Lord, Jerusalem.*

Matthew 5:17-19 "…till heaven and earth disappear, not one dot, not one little stroke, shall disappear from the Law until its purpose is achieved" (Matthew 5:18).

Jesus is the Teacher of the People of God. He is likewise the First among those who observe, and teach others to observe, all that comes from God and is destined for man (cf. Mt 5:19): the rich heritage of the Old Covenant. The Law and the Prophets.

The source of this heritage is the God of the Covenant. The words coming from him "are spirit and life" (cf. Jn 6:63). They are the "words of eternal life" (cf. Jn 6:68). Eternal life is the Kingdom of God, the Kingdom of Heaven. Christ's words in the Sermon on the Mount show man the way that leads to this Kingdom:

The Covenant… the Kingdom… these are key expressions of the Gospel, of the whole Bible of the Revelation. God, who speaks to man - and who has spoken many times …through the prophets, …finally …through his Son (cf. Heb 1:1-2) - reveals himself, unveils his salvific design concerning man. Who is man?

Man, amidst all the visible universe, is a unique being. The Creator has given him the capacity to know the truth, and in particular the truth regarding good and evil. He has given him freedom: the ability to choose. He ought to choose what he knows to be the true good. Yet he can choose against that truth. He can do evil.

This is man. This is how he has stood in the Creator's sight from the beginning…

Against the background of this truth about man, about human freedom and conscience, the Psalmist explains, in today's liturgy, the importance of the Divine Law: "Thou hast commanded thy precepts to be kept diligently". Therefore: "Blessed are those …who walk in the law of the Lord. Blessed are those who keep his testimonies, who seek him with their whole heart" (Ps 118 [119]:4. 1-2).

The Divine Law expresses what is truly good, and thus must be the principle of human conduct. The greatness of the Law, its binding force, are united to the truth concerning the good. God has revealed this truth to man. He has even written it "in the hearts" of men who do not know Revelation, as St. Paul recalls in the Letter to the Romans (2:15). Every human law finds here the source of its moral force. It is right and just when it expresses a true norm concerning the good that ought to be realized in human conduct.

Today's liturgy directs us in a particular way to God as the Principle and Ultimate Fount of the true good. God is the first Fount of the Law. Whence the confirmation of the indestructible force of the Divine Law in the words of Jesus: "not an iota, not a dot, will pass from the law until all is accomplished" (Mt 5:19)…

When Jesus of Nazareth reveals to his listeners the deep meaning of the commandments: "you shall not kill," "you shall not commit adultery," "you shall not swear falsely," there is made manifest before our eyes the abundance of justice which matures man for the Kingdom of God, for the Kingdom of Heaven. *Homily, Rome, February 13, 1987*

Thursday of the Third Week of Lent

We must stand by Christ

Readings of the day
Jeremiah 7:23-28 *This is the nation that will not listen to the voice of the Lord God.*
Psalm 94 *If today you hear his voice, harden not your hearts.*

Luke 11:14-23 "...he who does not gather with me, scatters" (Luke 11:23).

Let us then ask ourselves today what these words mean for us assembled here. The Lenten period is not for us a time of catechumenate in the strict sense of the word. In general we received the Sacrament of Baptism in the very first days of our lives, well before reaching the age of reason and thus before becoming aware of the fundamental importance of this sacrament.

Before receiving baptism we were catechumens", but we did not experience that which from the beginnings of the Church was - and continues to be - the catechumenate in the proper sense of the word. In a certain sense, could one say that this catechumenate was "postponed" to a later time in our lives - postponed to the period of preparation for our first Holy Communion, or for confirmation? To a degree, yes, but not exclusively. We must fulfill throughout our entire lives that which in the Christian tradition is the preparation for baptism. From this standpoint, the period of Lent is a privileged time. Already on Ash Wednesday this exhortation resounded during Mass: " ...we entreat you not to accept the grace of God in vain. Behold, now is the acceptable time; behold, now is the day of salvation" (2 Cor 6:2). This evening Christ says, "he who does not gather with me scatters."

We are called, then, to "gather with Christ." What does this mean?

To "gather" with Christ means to enter deeply into his paschal mystery, which is at the same time a mystery of the redemption of the world, of our redemption. We must rediscover this mystery in him - and simultaneously within ourselves.

The redemption is inscribed in the whole of human history. At the same time it is inscribed in the very humanity of each one of us. Man is in a certain sense the unceasing path of this mystery, which manifests itself and acts through the work of the Holy Spirit.

" …It is by the Spirit of God that I cast out demons" - says Christ - by "the finger of God"; and the Spirit, too, is referred to as "the finger": *digitus paternae dexterae.*

This, then, is the objective: to rediscover oneself on the forty-day journey of fasting - to rediscover oneself on the path of the mystery of the redemption. Yes! To rediscover oneself! Christ "reveals" man to himself - as the Council teaches, he indicates to man his true and definitive vocation. To "gather with Christ" means to discover this vocation: to identify ourselves with it, and to do so against the background of the whole struggle between good and evil, which invades the world.

Now we likewise understand the reason for the sacraments. We understand why baptism is at the beginning of our "gathering with Christ". We also understand the reason for the Sacrament of Penance, especially now during Lent! Why go to Confession? To "gather with Christ" means constantly to return, to turn back from "scattering". "He who does not gather with me scatters." *Homily, Rome, March 26, 1987*

Friday of the Third Week of Lent

Love is the foundation

Readings of the day
Hosea 14:2-10 *We will not say to the work of our hands: our God.*
Psalm 80 *I am the Lord, your God: hear my voice.*

Mark 12:28-34 "…and you shall love the Lord your God with all your heart, and with all your soul, and with all your mind, and with all your strength" (Mark 12:30).

The Apostle John wrote that God is love; it is he, not we, who loved first, and whoever loves abides in God and God in him (cf 1 John 4:16.19)…

A scribe asks Jesus: "Which is the first of all the commandments?" Jesus answers by quoting the passage from Deuteronomy …It is a very ancient text, which Jesus repeats and confirms in its entirety: "The Lord our God is Lord alone. You shall love the Lord your God with all your heart, with all your soul, with all your mind, and with all your strength" (Deut 6:4). This is a commandment, indeed the first commandment. However, it is valid to ask if one can really command love. If we take into consideration human psychology, love cannot be commanded, but arises spontaneously as a response when a person feels loved, or when the heart comes across a "unique" being.

This means that God is not only one, but he is also "unique". No one is as great, generous and tender as he is; no one is filled with goodness and is as loving as he is.

Jesus calls God "Father": his Father and our Father. However, in Sacred Scripture God is also presented as a Friend, as the Bridegroom, as the one who loves his people and each member of his people with an endless love.

This loving nature of God is proper to the Father, Son and Holy Spirit, that is, to the three Persons in one God. Thus, the commandment which today's Gospel speaks of, invites us to know and recognize this quality of the one God, so that every person can turn spontaneously to him with all his mind, all his heart and all his strength, live in constant orientation towards him, and love him as a Father, Friend and Bridegroom.

Jesus, however, did not stop at this passage from Deuteronomy. He added another phase, one taken from the Book of Leviticus (cf. Lev 19:18), saying: "The second (commandment) is this: 'You shall love your neighbour as yourself'". Then he added: "There is no other commandment greater than these".

The first and second commandments, love of God and neighbour, therefore, create a synthesis of all the commandments. Whoever loves God cannot but love those whom God loves, that is, all human beings, excluding no one.

Love of God and neighbour has changed the world. If today mankind is able to affirm the value of every human person, each person's right to life, respect and a just treatment, if people recognize the duty of cooperation and solidarity, it is because, following Jesus' teaching, a whole array of saints …dedicated their lives to the love of God and neighbour, convinced that the civilization of love must be the true goal of human history.
Homily, November 3, 1991

Saturday of the Third Week of Lent

The building of holiness rests on humility

Readings of the day

Hosea 5:15-6:6 *What I want is love not sacrifice.*

Psalm 50 *It is steadfast love, not sacrifice, that God desires.*

Luke 18:9-14 "Every one who exalts himself will be humbled, but he who humbles himself will be exalted" (Luke 18:14).

In fact, humility is truth. The first fundamental truth is the absolute transcendence of God the Creator, manifested in the infinite goodness of Christ the Redeemer: this is the supreme and decisive reality, in the face of which the person feels both exalted as a son and abased as a lowly creature who can boast of nothing.

Everything in the world teaches us this - our littleness in comparison to all the wonders of creation, our powerlessness in the face of all the terrible and overwhelming forces of nature. Science itself helps us to maintain this spirit of humility; considering the immensity of the universe which surrounds us, with its possibly expanding size and its multitudes of unconfined galaxies and planetary systems; meditating on the microcosm which is the atom, with all of its subatomic particles and cohesive forces, and on the organic wonder of the chromosomes, with the genes and chemical components which structure it; reflecting on the extraordinary actions and reactions of the neurons of the human brain, which serve the mind by helping it express thought, we logically arrive at the praise and admiration of that infinite Intelligence who created and ordered everything in such a harmonious and perfect way.

We cannot help but recognize our own total dependence on the Most High: true wisdom is just humility in front of God, and consequently a sense of adoration, of confidence in his love, of trust in his Providence, even when his designs may seem obscure and intricate.

The words of Sirach shine with the supreme wisdom: "My son, perform your tasks in meekness …The greater you are, the more you must humble yourself; so you will find favor in the sight of the Lord …he is glorified by the humble" (Sir 3:17-20).

History teaches us that unfortunately pride has been and still is the cause of infinite evil; even the denial of God and rebellion against him are almost always expressions of the rational being who thinks he is self-sufficient and does not want to bow before the omnipotent majesty of the Creator, nor accept the Mystery…

"For every one who exalts himself will be humbled, and he who humbles himself will be exalted" (Lk 14:11). This can already happen on this earth, in this life, but that is only secondary. What is essential is that the humble will be exalted in heaven by God himself. "Do you want to be great?" asks St. Augustine: and he answered: "Begin with the smallest things. Do you want to build a great building? First think about the foundation and the base" (Sermon 69, 1-2). If we truly desire to construct the building of our holiness, we must build its foundation on humility. *Homily, Anagni, August 31, 1986*

Fourth Sunday of Lent

Faith must win out over disbelief

Readings of the day
I Samuel 16:1. 6-7. 10-13 *In the presence of the Lord God, they anointed David king of Israel.*
Psalm 22 *The Lord is my shepherd; there is nothing I shall want.*
Ephesians 5:8-14 *Rise from the dead, and Christ will shine on you.*

John 9:1-41 "I am the light of the world" (John 9:5).

The event narrated in today's Liturgy shows us also that the faith of man, reborn through the power of Christ, encounters distrust and, indeed, incredulity.

In a certain sense, he must make his way through this distrust and incredulity. Thus does the faith of the man born blind, to whom Christ restored sight, make its way. His faith in the Son of Man encounters the opposition of the Pharisees, their incredulity. It is not easy for a socially disabled man to oppose this incredulity with his faith. Nevertheless, in the face of all the accusations that his questioners present against Jesus, he has an irrefutable argument: he restored my sight. "I was blind before; now I can see" (ibid., v.25).

Besides this resolute incredulity, the man cured of congenital blindness also encounters dread and fear, even on the part of his parents, who prefer not to expose themselves to the reprisals of the influential Pharisees: "We know this is our son, and we know he was blind at birth. But how he can see now, or who opened his eyes, we have no idea. Ask him. He is old enough to speak for himself" (ibid., vv. 21-22).

So, then, the faith of the man whose sight Christ restored goes through a difficult test but emerges victorious. The light which Christ instilled in his soul - not only in his eyes - is shown to be stronger than incredulity and distrust. It is revealed to be even stronger than human fears and the very intention to intimidate.

All this has its particular eloquence not only in the context of this concrete man and this concrete event (which in John's Gospel is described in an extraordinarily detailed manner), but also in the context of the life and the behavior of every man, of every Christian.

Is not the faith of each one of us exposed to our very weakness? - and also to incredulity, distrust, doubts, to pressure of opinions and, at times, to intimidation, discrimination and persecution?

We are thinking today of all the people in the whole world, all those to whom Christ has given his light; how much difficulty, oppression and persecution the faith of many of them is exposed to! And how often faith must battle with the weaknesses of every one of us! Let us pray for a strong faith. Let us pray for the courage of faith…

Faith creates a specific synthesis of light and strength of spirit, which come from God and which this Sunday's Liturgy emphasizes… A believing person accepts the light of Christ and at the same time, through the power of the Holy Spirit, becomes a sharer in Christ's threefold mission as prophet, priest and king. This sharing unites his life and his behavior with the salvific mission of the Good Shepherd, the mission addressed to all mankind and the whole world. The Good Shepherd is in fact the Redeemer of the world, and all those who through faith, hope and love belong to his fold, participate in the power of the mystery of the Redemption. *Homily, April 1, 1984*

Monday of the Fourth Week of Lent

Pray for the sick

Readings of the day
Isaiah 65:17-21 *No more will the sound of weeping or the sound of cries be heard.*
Psalm 29 *I will praise you, Lord, for you have rescued me.*

John 4:43-54 "...he went and begged him to come down and heal his son, for he was at the point of death" (John 4:47).

Uniting ourselves with Mary, a pilgrim in the faith, we are strengthened in the conviction that every second of life is a precious moment of grace that teaches us to welcome Christ as our sure hope.

In the Apostolic letter *Salvifici doloris*, ...I was able to observe that Mary most holy, "as a witness to her Son's passion by her presence, and as a sharer in it by her compassion, offered a unique contribution to the Gospel of suffering... She truly has a special title to be able to claim that she "completes in her flesh" as already in her heart "what is lacking in Christ's afflictions' " (n. 25).

At this moment, we are united in prayer and in offering our sufferings with all those who experience in their bodies the burden of sickness and the discomfort it causes...

Mary, who advances before the People of God on the pilgrimage of faith, goes before us all: in prayer, in thanksgiving, in supplication... A prayer that keeps us open to God's surprises including the surprise of suffering: a prayer that helps us live in a spirit of fraternal sharing... the great family of believers wishes to embrace with special affection every human family touched by suffering. These families, the small domestic Churches, are especially entrusted with welcoming all human life, healthy or ill from its beginning to its end. In addition the Christian family is open to the world: after the Virgin's example, it becomes a temple of God and sanctuary of the covenant, where the trustful offering of daily suffering, united with the Eucharistic sacrifice for the salvation of all mankind, finds its place. The knowledge of its own basic vocation, i.e. to be a way of communion in solidarity with those who suffer near and far, will never be lacking to the family that prays.

Beloved brothers and sisters, the silence of prayer allows us to hear Christ's inexpressible cry: the cry of those who "in their flesh are filling up what is lacking in the afflictions of Christ" (cf. Col 1:24).

How many are afflicted by all kinds of infirmities, especially children, the elderly, the defenseless and the victims of all kinds of human wickedness! Together with Christ they raise a "powerful cry" for the world and the great evils that pervade it. It is a cry for the victory of love over hatred, of peace over war; it is a forceful voice that is raised for justice and peace...

"Together with Mary, Mother of Christ, who stood beneath the cross (cf. Jn 19:25), we pause beside all the crosses of contemporary man" (*Salvifici doloris*, n. 31). We know that every pain united with the Redeemer's cross is a source of strength for the Church and for humanity.

May the Immaculate Conception, "Health of the Sick", guide us, protect us and console us. Amen. *Homily, February 11, 1994*

Tuesday of the Fourth Week of Lent

Lay people bring Christ to each person

Readings of the day
Ezekiel 47:1-9. 12 *I saw water coming forth from the temple, and all those were saved to whom water came.*
Psalm 45 *The mighty Lord is with us; the God of Jacob is our refuge.*

John 5:1-3. 5-16 "I have no man to put me into the pool when the water is troubled" (John 5:7).

God brought himself close to men. "And the Word was made flesh" (Jn 1:14). He came to live among us. He wants to dwell in everything that men are and accomplish. If he has entrusted a special mission to his disciples the pastors, nonetheless the Lord "also desires that his kingdom be spread by the lay faithful: the kingdom of truth and life, the kingdom of holiness and grace, the kingdom of justice, love and peace" (*Lumen Gentium*, n. 36).

Every day we ask in the Lords Prayer: "Thy Kingdom come". It is the first thing Jesus expects of those he has sent out: that they pray to the Father for the coming of his Kingdom as he himself prays… And a prayer offered in this way cures man of the illusion of thinking that he alone is responsible for this Kingdom. No one could carry the concern for the Kingdom of God under his own power without being crushed by it. Jesus tells us: "Ask it of the Father". Whoever prays in this way harmonizes himself with Gods initiative. The Our Father is the pre-eminent prayer of every committed Christian.

But the Lord willed to need men that his kingdom might be established, that creation might give glory to God; that his revealed truth might become known; that his love might be at work in every meeting between men, in every social relationship, in every family and in all associated life; that his Spirit might penetrate the furthest communities, and even the most resistant structures; that doors might be opened wide to his salvific action.

And here, dear brothers and sisters, you laity have an irreplaceable role. …You participate in the salutary mission of the Church. You are delegated to this apostolate by virtue of your Baptism, of your Confirmation (cf. ibid., n. 33). Members of the Body of Christ, you participate in his priestly function, making yourselves a spiritual offering with Christ. Through your explicit profession of faith and the witness of your life animated by the faith, you participate in his prophetic function; it is your way of making Christ known to others. You participate in his royal function, that the world might be freed from sin and imbued by the Spirit of Christ. It is through you, in a certain sense, that Christ listens to the joys and the sorrows of his brothers; that he loves them, encourages, them, walks with them. You are witnesses as well as living instruments of the Church's mission, at the height of Christ's gift. In particular, you assure the presence and the action of the Church in all the places and situations in which only through you can she become the salt of the earth and the light of the world (cf. ibid., n. 33). …Your fields of activity are diverse and complementary. The ecclesial communities need you in order that - in collaboration with the pastors and with respect for their sacred ministry - they may be assured of all those services that will permit a deepening of the faith, an expression of prayer, an expansion of charity. I therefore encourage those among you who collaborate in welcoming others, in the liturgy, in preparation for the sacraments, in youth and adult catechism, in approaching those who are furthest from the Church, in aiding the sick, the elderly, the immigrants, in missionary work, in the development of the Third World. *Homily, Antwerp (Belgium), May 17, 1985*

Wednesday of the Fourth Week of Lent

Work and family: a share in God's activity

Readings of the day
Isaiah 49:8-15 *I have given you as covenant of the people to establish the land.*
Psalm 144 *The Lord is kind and merciful.*

John 5:17-30 "My Father is working still and I am working" (John 5:17).

The figure of the carpenter of Nazareth, the husband of the Mother of God and the guardian of the Son of the Most High, is filled with meaning for the Church, the community called to live fully the mystery of mankind, a fullness which, as the Second Vatican Council affirmed, is fulfilled only in Christ. Thus the Mother of Jesus and St. Joseph in a special way draw the mystery of the Incarnate Word closer to the fundamental problems of human existence.

In substance it is a question of two realities: the family and work, not two realities which are distinct, but which are rather connected to one another in a close, mutual relationship.

This was the life in Nazareth during those 30 years which the evangelist summed up in the phrase: "Jesus went down with them (Mary and Joseph) and came to Nazareth and was subject to them" (Lk 2:51).

A brief expression, however, that emphasises quite well the bond that exists between the family and work…

The family and work! In the light of the Gospel and the Church's tradition, which are expressed not only in the continuity of her teaching but also in the Christian practice of life and morality, these two important human realities shed light on the proper hierarchy of values; they emphasize that the primacy belongs to the human being as a person and as a community of persons: in the first place, therefore, to the family.

All work, and especially physical labor, binds the person to the world of things, to the whole "order" of things. The world has been given to mankind as a task by the Creator, as an earthly job: "Subdue the earth!" The words from the Book of Genesis (cf. 1:28) indicate precisely this subordination of things to the person. The visible world is "for man". Things are for people.

May this order be understood and respected! May it never be violated, and even less so upset! Modern progress, as can be clearly seen, has such a danger in itself. The "progressive" culture, with the exception of those projects which have the person as their true reference, all too easily becomes a culture of things rather than of people. There are so many things that can be done, the calls of advertising and publicity are so insistent, that there is the risk of being overcome. People can end up being, even against their will, slaves of things and of the desire for possessions. Does not perhaps so-called consumerism represent the expression of "order" (or rather of "disorder") in which "having" is more important than "being"? …You are not slaves to selfish possession, but servants of sharing in solidarity! Fix the eyes of your spirit on the holy family and through the intercession of St. Joseph draw the determination that is enlightened by faith, courage and perseverance in goodness! *Homily, Fabriano (Italy), March 19, 1991*

Thursday of the Fourth Week of Lent

Open yourselves to the truth

Readings of the day
Exodus 32:7-14 *Relent, Lord, and do not bring disaster on your people.*
Psalm 105 *Lord, remember us for the love you bear your people.*

John 5:31-47 "I have come in my Father's name, yet you do not accept me" (John 5:43).

Today the words of the Gospel according to John introduce us to one of the moments of that dispute which Christ conducted with his contemporaries on the authenticity of his messianic mission. The action develops against the background of the cure of a lame man near the pool of Bethesda. This cure, done on the Sabbath, provoked a reaction on the part of the observers of the Mosaic Law. Jesus defends the correctness of his work - sustaining that the power of God himself, which cannot be limited by the letter of the Law, is manifested in it. This very power of God himself renders testimony to Christ.

"If I witness on my own behalf, you cannot verify my testimony; but there is another who is testifying on my behalf, and the testimony he renders me I know can be verified" (Jn 5:31-32)...

We find ourselves at the very center of that dispute which Jesus of Nazareth carries on with his contemporaries, representatives of Israel. They themselves, more than any others, could recognize in Christ the testimony of God himself. In fact, they were particularly prepared for this. Christ says "Search the Scriptures in which you think you have eternal life - they also testify on my behalf. Yet you are unwilling to come to me to possess that life" (ibid. 39-40)...

In today's Lenten liturgy of the Word of God, there unfolds, therefore, a dispute over the messianic content itself of Christ's mission.

Should we perhaps stop with this? Should we recognize this sort of argument only as a splendid event which pertains to the past, just as Moses' argument with the people, whose leader he was in the desert, pertains to an even more remote past?

No. We cannot stop here... The liturgical text always makes us pass from the past to the present....In fact, does not Christ - here and now, that is, in our era, in our generation - argue with man, with each one in a different way, about the messianic content of his mission? Does not the God of Revelation argue in Christ, who is "the same yesterday, today and forever" (Heb 13:8), with every man about the acceptance of the entire truth of this...

In an era in which the world seems to be closed in on itself and man is closed in within the world, ripping his own existence up from the fundamental sources of its meaning, Christ seems to say with a new force: "I have come in my Father's name, yet you do not accept me. But let someone come in his own name and him you will accept. How can people like you believe, when you accept praise from one another yet do not seek the glory that comes from the one God?" (Jn 5:43-44).

So, dear brothers and sisters, in this Lenten meditation we touch the deepest points of our relationship with God in Jesus Christ. Let us pause on these most profound points. Let us open ourselves to the Truth of Divine Revelation. Let us confess our sins in the Sacrament of Penance. Let us unite with Christ in the Eucharist. Let us enter the blessed time of Easter. *Homily, March 17, 1983*

Friday of the Fourth Week of Lent

Jesus freely accepted suffering to redeem us

Readings of the day
Wisdom 2:1. 12-22 *Let us condemn him to a shameful death.*
Psalm 33 *The Lord is near to the broken hearted.*

John 7:1-2. 10. 25-30 "…no one laid hands on him, because his hour had not yet come" (John 7:30).

According to the Gospel narratives, the Lord had given the news of his sacrifice some time in advance in order to prepare his disciples for that great test. After Peter's profession of faith near Caesarea Philippi, Christ had revealed the Father's mysterious plan: "The Son of man must suffer greatly, and be rejected by the elders, the high priests and scribes, and be killed and rise after three days" (Mk 8:31).

The announcement was so unexpected that Peter refused to accept it; he was not able to understand the mystery of a suffering Messiah; when he had expressed his faith in Jesus, he believed in a Messiah bound for triumph and glory…

The Father's plan was clear in Jesus' eyes; the path of suffering and death was necessary. And suffering had to be not only physical, but also moral, on account of the rejection by the religious leaders, the hatred of the people, the flight of the disciples.

Jesus one day explained, without mincing words, the reason for his coming to earth: "The Son of Man has come… to give his life in ransom for many" (Mk 10:45; Mt 20:28). Thus the Cross was not an accident in the journey made by Jesus, but an element consciously willed for the redemption of humankind.

Why such a sad fate? To free the world from sin. The Father wished that the Son take on the weight of sin's consequences. This decision makes us understand the seriousness of sin, which cannot be minimized since its consequences are so ruinous. Sin, as an offense against God, could not be remedied except by a Man-God.

Thus the Son, who came as Saviour, offered the Father the perfect homage of reparation and love, and gained for humanity the remission of sins and the communication of divine life. This sacrifice occurred once and for all in human history, and has salvific value for all people of all times and places. It is the sacrifice which is renewed in every Eucharist…

In the crucified Saviour we contemplate him who sacrificed himself for our salvation. "No one has greater love than this, to lay down one's life for one's friends" (Jn 15:13).

This immolation is enlightening for all of us: it shows us that love reaches its summit through suffering. Since Christ wished to associate us with his redemptive mission, we too are called to share his Cross. Sufferings, which are not lacking in our lives, are destined to be united with the one sacrifice of Christ. *General Audience, April 11, 1990*

Saturday of the Fourth Week of Lent

The Holy Spirit reveals Christ to us

Readings of the day
Jeremiah 11:18-20 *I am like a trustful lamb, being led to the slaughter.*
Psalm 7 *Lord, my God, I take shelter in you.*

John 7:40-52 "No man ever spoke like this man!" (John 7:46).

Already in the infancy narrative, when it is said of Jesus that "the grace of God was upon him", (Lk 2:40), the sanctifying presence of the Holy Spirit is indirectly shown. However, it is from the moment of the baptism in the Jordan that the Gospels speak more explicitly of Christ's activity in the power of the Spirit: "The Spirit immediately drove him out into the wilderness...", Mark says (Mk 1:12). In the desert, after a period of forty days fast, the Spirit of God permitted Jesus to be tempted by the devil, as a result of which he gained his first messianic victory (cf. Lk 4:1-14). Also during his public life, Jesus showed the same power of the Holy Spirit in dealing with those possessed by the devil. He himself emphasized it with the words, "if it is by the Spirit of God that I cast out demons, then the kingdom of God has come upon you" (Mt 12:28). The conclusion of the whole messianic struggle against the forces of evil was the paschal event - the death on the cross and the resurrection of him who came from the Father in the power of the Holy Spirit.

Likewise, after the ascension, Jesus remained for his disciples "he whom God anointed with the Holy Spirit and with power" (Acts 10:38). They recalled that thanks to this power, the people, hearkening to Jesus' teaching, praised God and said, "A great prophet has arisen among us, and God has visited his people" (Lk 7:16). "No man ever spoke like this man" (Jn 7:46), and they testified that by virtue of this power, Jesus "performed mighty works and wonders and signs" (cf. Acts 2:22), and so all the crowd sought to touch him, "for power came forth from him and healed them all" (Lk 6:19). In all that Jesus of Nazareth, the Son of man, did and taught, the words of the prophet Isaiah (cf. 42:1) on the Messiah were fulfilled: "Behold my servant whom I have chosen, my beloved with whom my soul is well pleased. I will put my Spirit upon him…" (Mt 12:18).

This power of the Holy Spirit is manifested to the very depths in Christ's redemptive sacrifice and in his resurrection. Truly Jesus is the Son of God "whom the Father anointed and sent into the world" (cf. Jn 10:36). In obedience to the will of the Father, he offers himself to God through the Spirit as a spotless victim, and this victim purifies our conscience from dead works to serve the living God (cf. Heb 9:14). The same Holy Spirit - as the Apostle Paul testifies - "has raised Jesus from the dead" (Rom 8:11), and through this "rising from the dead" Jesus Christ receives the fullness of messianic power, and is definitively revealed by the Holy Spirit as "Son of God with power" (literally: "designated Son of God in power according to the Spirit of holiness by his resurrection from the dead" (Rom 1:4).

Therefore Jesus Christ, the Son of God, comes into the world by the work of the Holy Spirit, and as Son of man he fulfils completely his messianic mission in the power of the Holy Spirit. But if Jesus Christ acts through this power during the whole of his saving activity and finally in the passion and resurrection, then it is the Holy Spirit himself who reveals that Jesus is the Son of God. Thus today, thanks to the Holy Spirit, the divinity of the Son, Jesus of Nazareth, shines before the world. With this in mind St. Paul writes: "No one can say, 'Jesus is Lord', except in the Holy Spirit" (1 Cor 12:3). *General audience, August 5, 1987*

Fifth Sunday of Lent

We have hope in the future resurrection

Readings of the day

Ezekiel 37:12-14 *I shall put my spirit in you, and you will live.*
Psalm 129 *With the Lord there is mercy and fullness of redemption.*
Romans 8:8-11 *If the Spirit of him who raised Jesus from the dead is living in you, then he will give life to your own mortal bodies.*

John 11:1-45 "…everyone who lives and believes in me will never die" (Jn 11:25-26).

The liturgy of this Fifth Sunday of Lent could not offer us more consoling words. In fact, day after day the fear of death threatens our insuppressible desire for life. Held in check by such an inevitable prospect, people often do everything to erase it from their thoughts. But of what use is that? Death is always lying in wait. Jesus alone can free the human being from such a nightmare: mourning the death of his friend and calling him back to life in order to restore him to his loved ones, Jesus reveals himself as the Lord of life and true friend of man.

In the mystery of his death and resurrection, Christ reduced to powerlessness "the one who has the power of death, that is, the devil", and has thus liberated "those who through fear of death had been subject to slavery all their life" (Heb 2:14-15).

"I am the resurrection and the life… Do you believe this? The Lord asks this question of each of us today. In the profession of faith the Church has us to repeat: "We believe in the resurrection of the body and life everlasting". This is a basic truth that sometimes seems alien and incomprehensible to the culture of our age, a culture often closed to the sense of the transcendent, almost totally centered on temporal existence. But what is man if everything is to be resolved in the brief cycle of his biological life?

The Catechism of the Catholic Church, the mature fruit of the Second Vatican Council, states: "We firmly believe and hope that, as Christ is truly risen from the dead and lives forever, so too the just, after their death, will live forever with the risen Christ, and that he will raise them up on the last day. Like his resurrection, ours too will be the work of the Blessed Trinity: "If the Spirit of him who raised Jesus from the dead dwells in you, he who raised Christ from the dead will give life to your mortal bodies also, through his Spirit that dwells in you" (Rom 8:11; n. 989).

What a consoling hope, dear brothers and sisters, breaks into our life then! This shining truth of faith throws open before us a wonderful prospect: life beyond death! And it is in light of such a truth that our daily activity as human beings and believers takes on its meaning and full value…

This, dearly beloved, is the great gift which the Lord renews for us through his Passover: a new life, free from the slavery of the flesh and the disordinate attachment to the passing goods of this world. A life renewed and placed under the dominion of the Spirit, source of love, joy and peace. *Homily, March 28, 1993*

Monday of the Fifth Week of Lent

To live chastely

Readings of the day
Daniel 13:41-62 *Here I am about to die though I have done none of the things charged against me.*
Psalm 22 *Though I walk in the valley of darkness I fear no evil, for you are with me.*

John 8:1-11 "Neither do I condemn you; go and do not sin again" (John 8:11).

Chastity is the joyous affirmation of someone who knows how to live self-giving, free from any form of self-centered slavery. This presupposes that the person has learned how to accept other people, to relate with them, while respecting their dignity in diversity. The chaste person is not self-centered, not involved in selfish relationships with other people. Chastity makes the personality harmonious. It matures it and fills it with inner peace. This purity of mind and body helps develop true self-respect and at the same time makes one capable of respecting others, because it makes one see in them persons to reverence, insofar as they are created in the image of God and through grace are children of God, recreated by Christ who "called you out of darkness into his marvelous light" (1 Pet 2:9).

"Chastity includes an apprenticeship in self-mastery which is a training in human freedom. The alternative is clear: either man governs his passions and finds peace, or he lets himself be dominated by them and becomes unhappy" (Catechism of the Catholic Church, 2339). Every person knows by experience that chastity requires rejecting certain thoughts, words and sinful actions, as St. Paul was careful to clarify and point out (cf. Rom 1:18; 6:12-14; 1 Cor 6:9-11; 2 Cor 7:1; Gal 5:16-23; Eph 4:17-24; 5:3-13; Col 3:5-8; 1 Thes 4:1-18; 1 Tim 1:8-11; 4:12). To achieve this requires ability and an attitude of self-mastery, which are signs of inner freedom, of responsibility toward oneself and others. At the same time, these signs bear witness to a faithful conscience. Such self-mastery involves both avoiding occasions that might provoke or encourage sin as well as knowing how to overcome one's own natural instinctive impulses.

When the family is providing real educational support and encouraging the exercise of all the virtues, education for chastity is made easy and lacks inner conflicts, even if at certain times young people can experience particularly delicate situations. For some who find themselves in situations where chastity is offended against and not valued, living in a chaste way can demand a hard or even a heroic struggle. Nonetheless, with the grace of Christ, flowing from his spousal love for the Church, everyone can live chastely even if they find themselves in unfavorable circumstances.

The very fact that all are called to holiness, as the Second Vatican Council teaches, makes it easier to understand that everyone can be in situations where heroic acts of virtue are indispensable, whether in celibate life or marriage, and that in fact in one way or another this happens to everyone for shorter or longer periods of time. Therefore, married life also entails a joyous and demanding path to holiness. *Truth and Meaning of Human Sexuality, PCF, 17,18*

Tuesday of the Fifth Week of Lent

Keep learning from the Cross through prayer

Readings of the day
Numbers 21:4-9 *Whoever looks at the bronze serpent shall live.*

Psalm 101 *O Lord, hear my prayer, and let my cry come to you.*

John 8:21-30 "You are from below, I am from above… I always do what is pleasing to him" (John 8:23.29).

When you have lifted up the Son of Man, then you will know that I am he, and that I do nothing on my own authority, but speak as the Father has taught me" (Jn 8:28).

Christ refers to the Father as the ultimate source of the truth that he proclaims: "He who sent me is true, and I declare to the world what I have heard from him" (Jn 8:26).

And finally, "He who sent me is with me; he has not left me alone for I always do what is pleasing to him" (Jn 8:29).

We must learn to measure the problems of the world, and above all the problems of man, by the cross and resurrection of Christ.

To be Christian means to live in the light of Christ's Paschal Mystery. And to find in it a fixed reference point for what is in man, for what is among men, for what makes up the history of mankind and the world.

Looking at himself, man discovers also - as Christ says in the dialogue with the Pharisees - what is "from below" and what is "from above". Man discovers within himself (this is a constant experience) the man "from below" and the man "from above": not two men, but almost two dimensions of the same man, the man that is each one of us: of you, he, she…

And each one of us - if he looks carefully within himself with a critical eye, if he tries to see himself in truth - will be able to tell what in him belongs to the man "from below" and what belongs to the man "from above". He will be able to call it by name. He will be able to confess it.

And finally, in each one of us there is a certain spontaneous tendency from the man "from below" towards the man "from above". This is a natural aspiration. At least let us not smother it, let us not crush it within us.

It is an aspiration. If we cooperate with it, this aspiration develops and becomes the propelling force of our life.

Christ teaches us how to cooperate with it, how to develop and deepen what in man is "from above", and how to weaken and conquer what is "from below".

Christ teaches this to us with his Gospel and his personal example.

The cross becomes here a living measure. It becomes the reference point through which the life of millions of men passes from what in man is "from below" to what is "from above".

The first and basic method for this passage is prayer. When man prays, in a certain sense he spontaneously turns toward him who offers him the "from above" dimension. With that itself he moves from what in himself is "from below". Prayer is an interior movement. It is a movement that decides the development of the whole human personality, of the direction of life… My beloved! In the name of the Crucified and Risen, I beg you: pray! Love prayer! *Homily, March 30, 1982*

Wednesday of the Fifth Week of Lent

Unite freedom to truth

Readings of the day
Daniel 3:14-20. 24-25. 28 *He has sent his angels to rescue his servants.*
Psalm (Dan. 3:52-56) *Glory and praise forever.*

John 8:31-42 "The truth will make you free" (John 8:32).

To create the Kingdom of God means being with Christ. To create the unity that it must constitute in us and among us, means precisely: gathering (storing up!) together with him. This is the fundamental program of the Kingdom of God, which Christ in his discourse contrasts with the activity of the evil spirit in us and among us, which stakes its program on man's freedom, apparently unlimited. It flatters man with a freedom that is not characteristic of him. It flatters whole environments, societies and generations. It flatters to manifest in the end that this freedom is nothing but adapting oneself to coercion in manifold forms: the coercion of the senses and instincts, the coercion of the situation, the coercion of information and the various media of communication, the coercion of current patterns of thought, evaluation, and behavior, in which the fundamental question is passed over in silence: that is, whether this behavior, is good or bad, worthy or unworthy.

Gradually the program itself expresses judgments and pronouncements on good and on evil, not according to the true value of the works and questions, but according to advantages and circumstances, according to the "imperative" of enjoyment or of immediate success.

Is it still possible for man to wake up? Can he tell himself clearly that this "unlimited freedom" becomes, when all is said and done, slavery?

Christ does not flatter his listeners, he does not flatter man with the appearance of "unlimited" freedom. He says: "You will know the truth, and the truth will make you free" (Jn 8:32) - and in this way he affirms that freedom is given to man not only as a gift, but as a duty. Yes. It is given to each of us as that duty, in which I and each of you is given as a duty to himself. It is the duty in accordance with life. And it is not a possession, which can be used in any way whatsoever and can be "scattered".

This duty of freedom - a marvelous duty - is carried out according to the program of Christ and his Kingdom in the area of truth. To be free means achieving the fruits of truth, acting in truth. To be free also means knowing how to give in, to submit oneself to truth, and not to submit truth to oneself, to one's own desires, to one's own interests, to one's own circumstances. To be free - according to the program of Christ and his Kingdom - does not mean pleasure but toil: the toil of freedom. At the cost of this toil man "does not scatter", but together with Christ "gathers" and "stores up".

At the cost of this toil man also acquires in himself that unity which is characteristic of the Kingdom of God. And, at the same cost, marriages, families, environments and societies achieve a similar unity. It is the unity of truth with freedom. It is the unity of freedom with truth. *Homily, March 26, 1981*

Thursday of the Fifth Week of Lent

The joy of finding Christ in our lives

Readings of the day
Genesis 17:3-9 *He will be the father of a multitude of nations.*
Psalm 104 *The Lord remembers his covenant for ever.*

John 8:51-59 "...he saw it and was glad" (John 8:56).

"*Laetare, Jerusalem*" (Rejoice, Jerusalem!).

In this way the Church expresses her joy and, at the same time, calls us to it as the fruit of that spiritual work which is carried out during Lent.

Lent, more than any other period in the liturgical year, must be a time of commitment and spiritual effort. But precisely this effort, this toil, gives an occasion for joy. During Lent, the Church lives in the prospect of the joy of the Resurrection. [The] call to joy today also reminds us of this prospect; but the joy that comes from toil is even greater. We feel this joy whenever we overcome our spiritual laziness, faint-heartedness, and indifference. We always feel joy when we see that we are capable of demanding something from ourselves; that we are capable of giving something of ourselves to God and to our neighbor. Real spiritual joy is the joy that springs from toil, from effort.

Let the period of Lent stimulate us, therefore, to carry out our Christian duties. Let us find again the joy that participation in the Eucharist gives us. Let Sunday Mass become for us the climax of every week. Let us find again the joy that comes from repentance, from conversion, from this splendid sacrament of reconciliation with God, which Christ set up to re-establish peace in man's conscience. Let us undertake the spiritual effort that Lent demands of us in order to be capable of accepting with all the depth of the spirit this call of the Church: "*Laetare, Jerusalem.*" Angelus, March 25, 1979.

…In an austere and eloquent act the Church imposes ashes on our heads as a sign of Lent. …This sign recalls to each of us the truth expressed in the words of the Book of Genesis: "You are dust and unto dust you shall return" (cf. Gen 3:19).

At the same time, however, the Church repeats the words which Jesus of Nazareth pronounced at the beginning of his mission: "Convert and believe the Gospel" (Mk 1:15).

The Church directs these words to all believers, or rather to all people, because the gift of salvation is offered to all. The power of the redemption of Christ knows no frontiers.

But the heart must be opened to receive the gift of heaven. Sin blocks this opening because it closes the person within selfishness. Lent is the acceptable time for freeing oneself from these obstacles and preparing the heart for the joy of a deeper repeated meeting with Christ in the light of Easter.

May each person know how to take advantage of Lent! *General audience, February 24, 1990*

Friday of the Fifth Week of Lent

Jesus lives to accomplish the Father's will

Readings of the day
Jeremiah 20:10-13 *The Lord God is with me, a mighty hero.*
Psalm 17 *In my distress I called upon the Lord, and he heard my voice.*

John 10:31-42 "even though you do not believe me, believe the works" (John 10:38).

Jesus goes as far as to say, "I and the Father are one" (Jn 10:30). These words are regarded as blasphemous and provoke a violent reaction among his hearers, "They took up stones to stone him" (cf. Jn 10:31): In fact, the Mosaic law prescribed the death penalty for blasphemy (cf. Dt 13:10-11). Now it is important to recognize the existence of an organic link between the truth of this intimate union of the Son with the Father and the fact that Jesus-Son lives completely "for the Father". We know indeed that the whole life, the entire earthly existence of Jesus is constantly directed to the Father: it is given to the Father without reserve. While still only twelve years old, Jesus, son of Mary, had a precise awareness of his relationship with the Father, and he adopts an attitude consistent with his interior certainty. Therefore in reply to the remonstrance of his Mother, when together with Joseph they find him in the Temple after having sought him for three days, he says, "Did you not know I had to be in my Father's house?" (Lk 2:49). *General audience, July 15, 1987*

The final two [joyful] mysteries [of the Rosary], while preserving [the] climate of joy, already point to the drama to come. The Presentation in the Temple not only expresses the joy of the Child's consecration and the ecstasy of the aged Simeon; it also records the prophecy that Christ will be a "sign of contradiction" for Israel and that a sword will pierce his mother's heart (cf Lk 2:34-35). Joy mixed with drama marks the fifth mystery, the finding of the twelve-year-old Jesus in the Temple. Here he appears in his divine wisdom as he listens and raises questions, already in effect one who "teaches". The revelation of his mystery as the Son wholly dedicated to his Father's affairs proclaims the radical nature of the Gospel, in which even the closest of human relationships are challenged by the absolute demands of the Kingdom. Mary and Joseph, fearful and anxious, "did not understand" his words (Lk 2:50)…

The Our Father (recited in the Rosary) - After listening to the word and focusing on the mystery [of the Rosary], it is natural for the mind to be lifted up towards the Father. In each of his mysteries, Jesus always leads us to the Father, for as he rests in the Father's bosom (cf. Jn 1:18) he is continually turned towards him. He wants us to share in his intimacy with the Father, so that we can say with him: "Abba, Father" (Rom 8:15; Gal 4:6). By virtue of his relationship to the Father he makes us brothers and sisters of himself and of one another, communicating to us the Spirit which is both his and the Father's. Acting as a kind of foundation for the Christological and Marian meditation which unfolds in the repetition of the Hail Mary, the Our Father makes meditation upon the mystery, even when carried out in solitude, an ecclesial experience. *Rosarium Virginis Mariae, 20, 32*

The Rosary is my favorite prayer. A marvelous prayer! Marvellous in its simplicity and its depth. …Against the background of the words Ave Maria the principle events of the life of Jesus Christ pass before the eyes of the soul. The take shape in the complete series of the joyful, sorrowful and glorious mysteries, and they put us in living communion with Jesus through – we might say – the heart of his Mother. *Angelus, October 29, 1978*

Saturday of the Fifth Week of Lent

The Gospel is history and transcendent meaning

Readings of the day
Ezekiel 37:21-28 *I will make them into one nation…*
Psalm (Jeremiah 31:10-13) *The Lord will guard us, like a shepherd guarding his flock.*

John 11:45-56 "He prophesied that Jesus should die (for the nation, and not for the nation only, but) to gather into one the children of God who are scattered abroad" (John 11:52).

We profess our belief in the central truth of Jesus Christ's messianic mission: he is the Redeemer of the world through his death on the Cross. We profess it in the words of the Nicene-Constantinopolitan Creed, according to which Jesus Christ "for our sake was crucified under Pontius Pilate, suffered death and was buried". In professing this faith we commemorate Christ's death as an historical event, which, like his life, is made known to us by sure and authoritative historical sources. On the basis of these sources we can and we desire to know and understand the historical circumstances of that death, which we believe to have been "the price" of human redemption in all ages…

When Jesus claimed to have the power to forgive sins, the scribes regarded this as blasphemy, because only God has such power (cf. Mk 2:6). When he worked miracles on the Sabbath day, asserting that "the Son of man is Lord on the Sabbath" (Mt 12:8), the reaction was similar. Already from that time their intention to kill Jesus was evident (cf. Mk 3:6): "they sought to kill him, because he not only broke the Sabbath, but also called God his Father, making himself equal with God" (Jn 5:18). What else could be the meaning of the words: "Truly, truly, I say to you, before Abraham was, I Am" (Jn 8:58)? His hearers knew very well the meaning of that "I AM. Therefore Jesus again runs the risk of being stoned. This time, however, Jesus "hid himself, and went out of the temple" (Jn 8:59).

The fact that eventually brought things to a head and led to the decision to kill Jesus was the raising of Lazarus from the dead in Bethany. John's Gospel informs us that at the subsequent meeting of the Sanhedrin it was stated: "This man performs many signs. If we let him go on thus, every one will believe in him, and the Romans will come and destroy both our holy place and our nation". In view of these forecasts and fears Caiaphas, the high priest, said to them: "It is evident that one man should die for the people and that the whole nation should not perish" (Jn 11:47-50). The evangelist adds: "He did not say this of his own accord, but being high priest that year he prophesied that Jesus should die for the nation, and not for the nation only, but to gather into one the children of God who are scattered abroad". And he concludes: "So from that day on they took counsel how to put him to death" (Jn 11:51-53).

In this way John informs us of the twofold aspect of the position adopted by Caiaphas. From the human point of view, which could be more accurately described as opportunist, it was an attempt to justify the elimination of a man regarded as politically dangerous, without caring about his innocence. From a higher point of view, made his own and noted by the evangelist, Caiaphas' words, independently of his intention, had a truly prophetic content regarding the mystery of Christ's death according to God's salvific plan. *General audience, September 28, 1988*

Passion (Palm) Sunday

The palm of triumph and the cross of the Passion

Readings of the day

Gospel of the Procession: Matthew 21:1-11 *Blessed is he who comes in the name of the Lord*

Isaiah 50:4-7 *I did not cover my face against insult and I know I will not be ashamed.*

Psalm 21 *My God, my God, why have you abandoned me?*

Philippians 2:6-11 The Passion of Our Lord Jesus Christ according to Matthew (26:14-27:66).

"Behold, your king is coming to you, humble, and mounted on an ass, and on a colt , the foal of an ass" (Matthew 21:5 – Isaiah 62:11; Zechariah 9:9).

"Blessed is he who comes in the name of the Lord" (Mk11:9). The liturgy of Palm Sunday is like a formal entrance into Holy Week. It combines two contrasting moments: the welcome of Jesus in Jerusalem and the drama of the Passion; the festive "Hosanna" and the repeated cry to "Crucify him!"; the triumphal entry and the apparent defeat through death on the Cross. The liturgy thus anticipates the "hour" in which the Messiah was to suffer greatly, to be put to death, and on the third day to rise again (cf. Mt 16:21), and prepares us to live fully the paschal mystery.

"Rejoice, O daughter of Jerusalem! Behold, your king comes to you" (Zec 9:9). In welcoming Jesus, the city with the vivid memory of David rejoices; the city of the prophets, many of whom were to suffer martyrdom for the truth; the city of peace, which, down through the ages, has known violence, war and deportation.

In a certain way, Jerusalem can be considered the city-symbol of humanity, especially at this dramatic beginning of the third millennium that we are living. The Palm Sunday rites thus acquire a special eloquence of their own… Today we are cel-ebrating for today Jesus, the King of peace, enters Jerusalem.

Today, with faith and joy, we acclaim Christ who is our "King": the King of truth, freedom, justice and love. These are the four "pillars" on which it is possible to build true peace… Peace is the gift of Christ, which he obtained for us with the sacrifice of the Cross. To achieve it effectively it is necessary to climb with the divine Teacher up to Calvary. And who can guide us better in this ascent than Mary who, as she stood at the foot of the Cross, was given to us as our mother through the faithful apostle, St. John? …Accepting this testament of love, John opened his home to Mary (cf.Jn 19:27), that is, he welcomed her into his life, sharing with her a completely new spiritual closeness. The intimate bond with the Mother of the Lord will lead the "beloved disciple" to become the apostle of that Love that he drew from the Heart of Christ through the Immaculate Heart of Mary.

"Behold, your mother!" Jesus addresses these words to each of you, dear friends. He also asks you to take Mary as your mother "into your home", to welcome her "as one of yours", because "she will discharge her ministry as a mother and train you and model you until Christ is fully formed in you" (Message for WYD, n.3, 19 March 2003)

May Mary make it so that you respond generously to the Lord's call, and persevere with joy and fidelity in the Christian mission! O Mary, sorrowful Mother, you are a silent witness of these decisive moments for the history of salvation. Give us your eyes so that on the face of the crucified One, disfigured by pain, we may recognise the image of the glorious Risen One. Help us to embrace him and entrust ourselves to him, so that we be made worthy of his promises. Help us to be faithful today and throughout our lives. *Homily, April 13, 2003*

Monday of Holy Week

Be helpful to each who is near

Readings of the day
Isaiah 42:1-7 *He will not cry out, nor make his voice be heard in the streets.*
Psalm 26 *The Lord is my light and my salvation.*

John 12:1-11 "The poor you always have with you, but you do not always have me" (John 12:7-8).

The discreet words which Christ addressed one day to the traitor apostle ring out with unusual forcefulness: "The poor you always have with you, but you do not always have me." (Jn 12:8)

"You will always have poor people among you." After the abyss of these words, no man has ever been able to say what Poverty is... When God is questioned, he answers that it is precisely he who is the Poor Man: "*Ego sum pauper.*" (Leon Bloy, *La femme pauvre~.* 11. 1. *Mercure de France* 1948.)

The call to repentance, to conversion, means a call to interior opening "to others". Nothing in the history of the Church and in the history of man can replace this call. This call has infinite destinations. It is addressed to every man, and it is addressed to each one for reasons specific to each one. So everyone must see himself in the two aspects of the destination of this call. Christ demands of me an opening to the other. But to what other? To the one who is here, at this moment! It is not possible to "postpone" this call of Christ to an indefinite moment, in which that "qualified" beggar will appear and stretch out his hand. I must be open to every man, ready to "be helpful". Be helpful, how? It is well known that sometimes we can "make a present" to the other with a single word. But with a single word we can also strike him painfully, offend him, wound him; we can even "kill him" morally. It is necessary, therefore, to accept this call of Christ in those ordinary everyday situations of coexistence and contact where each of us is always the one who can "give" to others and, at the same time the one who is able to accept what others can offer him.

To realize Christ's call to open inwardly to others means living always ready to find oneself at the other end of the destination of this call. I am the one who gives to others even when I accept, when I am grateful for every good that comes to me from others. I cannot be closed and ungrateful. I cannot isolate myself. To accept Christ's call to opening to others requires, as can be seen, a re-elaboration of the whole style of our daily life. It is necessary to accept this call in the real dimensions of life; not postpone it to different conditions and circumstances, to the occasion when the necessity will present itself. It is necessary to persevere continually in this interior attitude. Otherwise, when that "extraordinary" opportunity turns up it may happen that we do not have an adequate disposition. *General Audience, April 4, 1979*

Tuesday of Holy Week

Do we love him?

Readings of the day
Isaiah 49:1-6 *I have made you the light of nations so that my salvation may reach to the ends of the earth.*
Psalm 70 *I will sing of your salvation.*

John 13:21-33. 36-38 "…the cock will not crow, till you have denied me three times" (John 13:38).

Do you love?

A fundamental question, a common question. It is the question that opens the heart - and that gives its meaning to life. It is the question that decides man's true dimension. In it, it is the whole man who must express himself, and who must also, in it, transcend himself…

This question was put to Peter by Christ. Christ asked it three times, and three times Peter answered. "Simon, son of John, do you love me? -Yes, Lord, you know that I love you" (Jn 21: 15-17)…

Peter can never detach himself from this question: "Do you love me?" He takes it with him wherever he goes. He takes it through the centuries, through the generations. In the midst of new peoples and new nations. In the midst of ever new languages and races. He alone takes it, and yet he is no longer alone. Others take it with him: Paul, John, James, Andrew, Irenneus of Lyons, Benedict of Norcia, Martin of Tours, Bernard of Clairvaux. The 'Poor Man' of Assisi, Joan of Arc, Francis of Sales, Jane Frances de Chantal, Vincent de Paul, John Mary Vianney, Therese of Lisieux.

On this land which I have the privilege of visiting today, here, in this city, there have been, and there are, my men and women who have known and who still know today that their whole life has a value and meaning solely and exclusively to the extent to which it is an answer to this same question: Do you love? Do you love me? They have given, and give, their answer in a complete and perfect way - a heroic answer - or else in a common, ordinary way. But in any case they know that their lives, that human life in general, has a value and a meaning to the extent to which it is the answer to this question: Do you love? It is only thanks to this question that life is worth living… The answer they have given to this question: "Do you love?" has a universal significance, an abiding value. It constructs in the history of mankind the world of good. Only love constructs this world. It constructs it with difficulty. It must struggle to give it shape: it must struggle against the forces of evil, sin, hatred, against the lust of the flesh, against the lust of the eyes and against the pride of life (cf. I Jn 2:16) …Christ is the cornerstone of this construction. He is the cornerstone of this shape that the world, our human world, can take thanks to love. Peter knew this, he whom Christ asked three times: "Do you love me?". Peter knew, he who, when put to the test, denied his Master three times. …It is from him that, in spite of all conflicts, objections and denials, in spite of the darkness and the clouds that continue to gather on the horizon of history - and you know how threatening they are today, in our age! -it is from him that the abiding construction will spring up, it is on him that it will take the shape of eternity in the earthly and short-lived dimensions of the history of man on the earth. *Homily, Paris, May 30, 1980*

Wednesday of Holy Week

Lest Christ be betrayed

Readings of the day
Isaiah 50:4-9 *I did not cover my face against insult and spittle.*
Psalm 68 *Lord, in your great love answer me.*

Matthew 26:14-25 "They paid him thirty pieces of silver. And from that moment he sought an opportunity to betray him" (Matthew 26:15-16).

Here let us consider the human development of the events. In that meeting of the Sanhedrin a decision was taken to kill Jesus of Nazareth. They took advantage of his presence in Jerusalem during the paschal feasts. Judas; one of the Twelve, betrayed Jesus for thirty pieces of silver, by indicating the place where he could be arrested. They seized Jesus and brought him before the Sanhedrin. To the vital question of the high priest: "I adjure you by the living God, tell us if you are the Christ, the Son of God. Jesus replied: "You have said so" (Mt 25:63-64; cf. Mk 14:62; Lk 22:70). In this statement the Sanhedrin saw an evident blasphemy, and decreed that Jesus was "guilty of death" (Mk 14:64). The Sanhedrin, however, could not carry out the sentence without the consent of the Roman procurator. Pilate is personally convinced that Jesus is innocent and indicates that several times. After having opposed an uncertain resistance to the pressures of the Sanhedrin, he at last gives in for fear of risking the disapproval of Caesar, all the more so because the crowd also, urged on by those in favour of Jesus' elimination, now cry out for his crucifixion. "Crucify him!" Thus Jesus is condemned to death by crucifixion.

Historical responsibility for Christ's crucifixion rests with those mentioned in the Gospels, at least in part, by name. Jesus himself says so when he says to Pilate during the trial: "He who delivered me to you has the greater sin" (Jn 19:11). In another passage also: "The Son of man goes as it is written of him, but woe to that man by whom the Son of man is betrayed! It would have been better for that man if he had not been born" (Mk 14: 21; Mt 26:24: Lk 22:22). Jesus alludes to various persons who, in different ways, will be responsible for his death: Judas, the representatives of the Sanhedrin, Pilate and the others... Simon Peter, also, in his discourse after Pentecost, will charge the leaders of the Sanhedrin with the killing of Jesus: "You crucified and killed him by the hands of lawless men" (Acts 2:23).

However, this accusation cannot be extended beyond the circle of people really responsible. We read in a document of the Second Vatican Council: "Even though the Jewish authorities and those who followed their lead pressed for the death of Christ, neither all Jews indiscriminately at that time, nor Jews today, can be charged with the crimes committed during his passion" (Declaration, *Nostra Aetate*, 4).

As for the consciences of those individuals who were responsible, we must remember Christ's words on the Cross: "Father, forgive them; for they know not what they do" (Lk 23:34). There is an echo of these words in another of Peter's discourses after Pentecost: "And now, brethren, I know that you acted in ignorance, as did also your rulers" (Acts 3:17). What a sense of reserve before the mystery of the human conscience, even in the case of the greatest crime committed in history, the killing of Christ!

Following the example of Jesus and Peter, even though it is difficult to deny the responsibility of those who deliberately brought about the death of Christ, we too shall view things in the light of God's eternal plan, which asked from his beloved Son the offering of himself as a victim for the sins of all mankind. In this higher perspective we realize that, because of our sins, we are all responsible for Christ's death on the cross: all of us, to the extent that through sin we have contributed to causing Christ's death for us as a victim of expiation. *General Audience, September 28, 1988*

Holy Thursday

The Eucharist is the mystery of faith and love

Readings of the day

Exodus 12:1-8. 11-14 *The law for the Passover meal.*
Psalm 115 *Our blessing cup is a communion with the blood of Christ.*
John 13:1-15 *To the end he showed his love for them.*

1 Corinthians 11:23-26 "This is my body which is for you. Do this in remembrance of me"(1 Corinthians 11:24).

"*Adoro te devote, latens Deitas, quae sub his figuris vere latitas*". "Devoutly I adore you, hidden Deity, under these appearances concealed".

This evening we re-live the Last Supper when, on the night he was betrayed, the divine Saviour left us the Eucharistic Sacrifice of his Body and his Blood, the memorial of his Death and Resurrection, a sacrament of love, a sign of unity and a bond of charity (cf. *Sacrosanctum Concilium*, n.47).

The readings of this celebration all speak of rites and actions destined to imprint upon history the saving plan of God. The Book of Exodus passes on the priestly document, which establishes the regulations for celebrating the Jewish Passover. The Apostle Paul, in his First Letter to the Corinthians, passes on to the Church the most ancient testimony of the new Christian paschal Supper: it is the rite of the new and everlasting Covenant, instituted by Jesus in the Upper Room before the Passion. Finally, John the Evangelist, enlightened by the Holy Spirit, summarises the profound meaning of Christ's immolation in the act of the "washing of the feet".

It is the Passover of the Lord, which is rooted in the history of the people of Israel and finds its fulfillment in Jesus Christ, the Lamb of God sacrificed for our salvation.

The Church lives by the Eucharist. Thanks to the ministry of the Apostles and their successors, in an uninterrupted series which begins in the Upper Room, Christ's words and actions are renewed, following the Church's journey, in order to offer the Bread of life to the men and women of each generation: "This is my body which is for you. Do this in remembrance of me... This cup is the new covenant in my blood. Do this, as often as you drink it, in remembrance of me"(1 Cor 11:24-24).

As a sacramental renewal of the sacrifice of the Cross, the Eucharist is the summit of the work of redemption: it proclaims and brings about that mystery which is the source of life for every person. In fact, every time we eat this bread and drink this cup, we proclaim the Lord's death until he comes"(cf.1 Cor 11:26).

After the consecration, the priest proclaims: *"Mysterium fidei"*, and the people respond "Christ has died, Christ is risen, Christ will come again".

Yes, today we are given to understand in a special way that the "mystery of the faith" is truly great, and the simplicity of the Eucharistic symbols – the bread and wine – serve only to give greater emphasis to its depth....

The life-giving power of Christ's death! The purifying power of Christ's blood which obtains the forgiveness of sins for the people of all times and all places. The sublimeness of the redemptive sacrifice... This mystery of love, "incomprehensible" to the human being, is offered in its entirety in the sacrament of the Eucharist. Christians are invited to pause before it this evening, even late into the night, in silent adoration... This is the Church's faith. This is the faith of each one of us before the sublime Eucharistic mystery. Yes, may words cease and adoration endure. In silence. *Homily, Holy Thursday, April 1, 1999*

Good Friday

It is consummated

Readings of the day
Isaiah 52:13. 53:12 *He surrendered himself to death, while bearing the faults of many.*
Psalm 30 *Father, I put my life in your hands.*
Hebrews 4:14-16; 5:7-9 *He learned obedience and became the source of eternal salvation for all who obey him.*

The Passion of Our Lord Jesus Christ according to John (18:1 – 19:42) "It is consummated" (John 19:30).

In contemplating Christ's face, we confront the most paradoxical aspect of his mystery, as it emerges in his last hour, on the Cross. The mystery within the mystery, before which we cannot but prostrate ourselves in adoration.

The intensity of the episode in the Garden of Olives passes before our eyes. Oppressed by foreknowledge of the trials that await him, and alone before the Father, Jesus cries out to him in his habitual and affectionate expression of trust: "Abba, Father". He asks him to take away, if possible, the cup of suffering (cf.Mk 14:36). But the Father seems not to want to heed the Son's cry. In order to bring man back to the Father's face, Jesus not only had to take on the face of man, but he had to burden himself with the "face" of sin. "For our sake he made him to be sin who knew no sin, so that in him we might become the righteousness of God"(2 Cor 5:21)."

We shall never exhaust the depths of this mystery. All the harshness of the paradox can be heard in Jesus' seemingly desperate cry of pain on the Cross: "'*Eloi, Eloi, lama sabachtani*' which means: 'My God, my God, why have you forsaken me?'"(Mk 15:34). Is it possible to imagine a greater agony, a more impenetrable darkness? In reality, the anguished "why" addressed to the Father in the opening words of the Twenty-second Psalm expresses all the realism of unspeakable pain; but it is also illumined by the meaning of that entire prayer, in which the Psalmist brings together suffering and trust, in a moving blend of emotions. In fact the Psalm continues: "in you our fathers put their trust; they trusted and you set them free... Do not leave me alone in my distress; come close, there is none else to help"(Ps 22:5, 12).

Jesus' cry on the Cross, dear brothers and sisters, is not the cry of anguish of a man without hope, but the prayer of the Son who offers his life to the Father in love, for the salvation of all. At the very moment when he identifies with our sin, "abandoned by the Father", he "abandons" himself in the hands of the Father. *Novo millennio ineunte, 25,26*

"*In manus tuas, Domine, commendo spiritum meum*"; "Father, into your hands I commit my spirit". These are the words, this is the last cry of Christ on the Cross. It is these words that close the mystery of the Passion and open up the mystery of liberation through death, which will be fulfilled in the Resurrection. They are important words. The Church, aware of their importance, has incorporated them into the Liturgy of the Hours and every day ends it with these words: "Into your hands, Lord, I commend my spirit".

Today we would like to put these words on humanity's lips... They signify openness to the future. ...We hope that at the end of this Good Friday, and Easter Vigil ...the words "Father, into your hands I commit my spirit" – will be the last words for us, those which will open eternity to us. *Homily, Good Friday, April 2, 1999*

Holy Saturday

Mary helps us be faithful

Readings of the day
This is the only non-liturgical day of the Church's year. There are no assigned readings.

"Behold your Mother" (John 19:27).

On Holy Saturday the Church is, as it were, at the Lord's tomb, meditating on his passion and death, and on his descent into hell, and awaiting his resurrection with prayer and fasting. It is highly recommended that on this day the Office of Readings and Morning Prayer be celebrated with the participation of the people (cf. n. 40). (76) Where this cannot be done, there should be some celebration of the Word of God, or some act of devotion suited to the mystery celebrated this day.

The image of Christ crucified or lying in the tomb, or the descent into hell, which mystery Holy Saturday recalls, as also an image of the sorrowful Virgin Mary can be placed in the church for the veneration of the faithful.

On this day the Church abstains strictly from the celebration of the sacrifice of the Mass. Holy Communion may only be given in the form of Viaticum. The celebration of marriages is forbidden, as also the celebration of other sacraments, except those of Penance and the Anointing of the Sick… *Paschales Solemnitatis*, 73-75

Holy Saturday is the day when the Church contemplates Christ resting in the tomb after the victorious baffle of the Cross. She commemorates his descent into the world of death to heal humanity's roots, and waits for his promise to be fulfilled: "The Son of Man will be delivered to the chief priests and the scribes, and they 'will condemn him to death and deliver him to the Gentiles; and they kill him; and after three days he will rise" (Mk 10:33-34).

An ancient author describes the mystery of Holy Saturday with words full of faith and poetry: 'Today there is a great silence over the earth, a great silence and stillness, a great silence because the King sleeps; the earth was in terror and was still, because God slept in the flesh and raised up those who were sleeping from the ages. God has died in the flesh, and the underworld has trembled'. The text then continues, describing Christ's conversation with Adam: 'I am your God, who for your sake became your son, who for you and your descendants now speak and command with authority those in prison: Come forth, and those in darkness: Have light, and those who sleep: Rise. I command you: Awake, sleeper, I have not made you to be held a prisoner in the underworld. Arise from the dead; I am the life of the dead. Arise, O man, work of my hands, arise, you who were fashioned in my image… The enemy brought you out of the land of paradise; I will reinstate you, no longer in paradise, but on the throne of heaven… The kingdom of heaven has been prepared for you before the ages" *(Office of Readings for Holy Saturday; PG 43:439, 451, 462463).*

On Holy Saturday the Church is once again identified with Mary: all her faith comes together in her, the first believer. In the darkness that envelops creation, she alone remains to keep alive the flame of faith, preparing to receive the joyful and astonishing announcement of the Resurrection. In remembering the Mother of the Lord, the Christian community is called on this a-liturgical day to dedicate itself to silence and meditation and, in its waiting, to foster the blessed hope of the renewed encounter with its Lord. *General audience April 3, 1996*

Easter Vigil

Night of faith and hope

> **Readings of the day** *(up to seven from the Old Testament, each with a psalm, e.g.)*
>> **Genesis 1:1-2:2 and Psalm 103** *Lord, send out your Spirit and renew the face of the earth.*
>> **Genesis 22:-18 and Psalm 15** *Keep me safe, O God; you are my hope.*
>> **Exodus 14:15. 15:1 and Exodus 15** *Let us sing to the Lord; he has covered himself in glory.*
>> **Ezekiel 36:16-28 and Psalms 41,42** *Like a deer that longs for running streams, my soul longs for you, my God.*
>> **Romans 6:5-11** *Christ, having been raised from the dead, will never die again.*
>> **Psalm 117** *Alleluia. Alleluia. Alleluia.*
>
> **Matthew 28:1-10 or Mark 16:1-7 or Luke 24:1-12 "Do not be afraid…" (Matthew 28:5).**

The tomb of Jesus had been closed and sealed. At the request of the Chief Priests and the Pharisees, soldiers were placed on guard. Lest anyone steal the body (cf.Mt 27: 63-64). This is the event from which the liturgy of the Easter Vigil begins.

Those who had sought the death of Christ, those who considered him an "imposter" (Mt 27:63), were keeping watch beside the tomb. They wanted him and his message to be buried forever.

Not far away, Mary was keeping watch, and with her the Apostles and a few women. In their hearts they pondered the distressing events which had just taken place.

The Church keeps watch this night, in every corner of the world, and she relives the principal stages of salvation history. The solemn liturgy, which we are celebrating, is the expression of this "keeping watch" which, in a way, evokes the watch kept by God himself… As she keeps watch on this Holy Night, the Church closely scrutinises the texts of Sacred Scripture. They portray God's plan from Genesis to the Gospel and, together with the liturgical rites of fire and water, give this remarkable celebration a cosmic dimension. The whole, created universe is summoned to keep watch this night at the tomb of Christ. The history of salvation passes before our eyes, from Creation to the Redemption, from the Exodus to the Covenant on Mount Sinai, from the Old to the New and Eternal Covenant. On this Holy Night, God's eternal plan reaches fulfillment, the plan which embraces the history of humanity and of the cosmos.

At the Easter Vigil, "the mother of all vigils", everyone can likewise acknowledge their own personal history of salvation, which has its basic moment in our rebirth in Christ through Baptism…

The tomb! Behold the place where they buried him (cf. Mk 16:6). There the community of the Church throughout the world is spiritually present. We too are there with the three women going to the tomb before dawn to anoint the lifeless body of Jesus (cf. Mk 16:1). Their loving concern is our concern too. With them we discover that the large tombstone has been rolled away and that the body is no longer there. "He is not here", the angel proclaims, pointing to the empty tomb and the winding cloth on the ground. Death no longer has power over him (cf. Rom 6:9).

"Christ is risen from the tomb, who for our sakes hung upon the Cross, Alleluia!" …Yes, Christ is truly risen and we are witnesses of this. We proclaim this witness to the world, so that the joy which is ours will reach countless other hearts, kindling in them the light of the hope which does not disappoint. Christ is risen, alleluia! *Christos anesti, alleluia! Homily, Easter Vigil, April 22, 2000*

Easter Sunday

All is new in Jesus who has risen!

Readings of the day
Acts of the Apostles 10:34. 37-43 *We have eaten and drunk with him after his resurrection from the dead.*
Psalm 117 *This is the day the Lord has made; let us rejoice and be glad!*
Colossians 3:1-4 *Look for the things that are in heaven, where Christ is.*

John 20:1-9 "…the other disciple who had reached the tomb first also went in; he saw and he believed" (John 20:8).

"In the Risen Christ all creation rises to new life!" May the Easter proclamation reach all the peoples of the earth, and may all people of good will feel themselves called to an active role on this day which the Lord has made, the day of his resurrection, when the Church, filled with joy, proclaims that the Lord is truly risen. This cry which bursts forth from the hearts of the disciples on the first day after the Sabbath has spanned the centuries and now, at this precise moment of history, renews once more humanity's hopes with the unaltered certainty of the Resurrection of Christ, the Redeemer of mankind.

"In the Risen Christ all creation rises to new life". The amazed surprise of the Apostles and the women who rushed to the tomb at sunrise today becomes the shared experience of the whole People of God. As the new millenium begins its course we wish to hand on to the younger generation the certitude that is basic to our lives: Christ is risen and in him all creation rises to new life. "Glory to you, O Christ Jesus, today and always you will reign". We are reminded of this faith-filled hymn, which we sang so many times during the course of the Jubilee praising him who is "the Alpha and the Omega, the first and the last, the beginning and the end" (Rv 22:13). To him the pilgrim Church remains faithful "amid the world's persecutions and God's consolations" (St. Augustine). She looks to him and has no fear. She walks with her gaze fixed on his face, and repeats to the men and women of our day that he, the Risen One, is "the same yesterday and today and for ever" (Heb 13:8)…

On this day heaven and earth sing out the ineffable and sublime "name" of the Crucified One who has risen. Everything appears as before, but in fact nothing is the same as before. He, the Life that does not die, has redeemed every human life and reopened it to hope. "The old has passed away, behold, the new has come" (cf. 2 Cor 5:17). Every project and plan of this noble and frail creature that is man has a new "name" today in Christ risen from the dead, for "in him all creation rises to new life". The words of Genesis are fully fulfilled in this new creation: "Then God said: 'Let us make man in our image after our likeness" (Gn 1:26). At Easter, Christ, the new Adam, having become "a life-giving spirit" (1 Cor 15:45), ransoms the old Adam from the defeat of death.

Men and women of the third millennium, the Easter gift of light that scatters the darkness of fear and sadness is meant for everyone; all are offered the gift of the peace of the Risen Christ who breaks the chains of violence and hatred. Rediscover today with joy and wonder that the world is no longer a slave to the inevitable. This world of ours can change: peace is possible even where for too long there has been fighting and death…

Men and women of every continent, draw from his tomb, empty now for ever, the strength needed to defeat the powers of evil and death, and to place all research and all technical and social progress at the service of a better future for all… You, victorious King, grant to us and to the world eternal salvation!

Easter Sunday, 15 April, 2001

Index of Themes

Acknowledgments

The English translation of the captions for the readings and the psalm responses from lectionary for Mass ©1969, 1981, 1997, International Committee on English in the Liturgy, Inc. All rights reserved.

The writings of the Holy Father John Paul II are taken from L'Osservatore Romano. Cover © L'Osservatore Romano.